P9-CME-074

On Treason

ALSO BY CARLTON F. W. LARSON

The Trials of Allegiance: Treason, Juries, and the American Revolution

On Treason

A CITIZEN'S GUIDE *to the* LAW

CARLTON F. W. LARSON

ecco
An Imprint of HarperCollins*Publishers*

 For information, address HarperCollins Publishers, 195 Broadway, New York, NY 10007.

HarperCollins books may be purchased for educational, business, or sales promotional use. For information, please email the Special Markets Department at SPsales@harpercollins.com.

FIRST EDITION

Designed by Angela Boutin

Frontispiece © Reddavebatcave/Shutterstock.com

Library of Congress Cataloging-in-Publication Data has been applied for.

ISBN 978-0-06-299616-9

20 21 22 23 24 LSC 10 9 8 7 6 5 4 3 2 1

To Elaine, Carina, and Elliot

Treason against the United States, shall consist only in levying War against them, or in adhering to their Enemies, giving them Aid and Comfort. No person shall be convicted of Treason unless on the Testimony of two Witnesses to the same overt Act, or on Confession in open Court.
The Congress shall have Power to declare the Punishment of Treason, but no Attainder of Treason shall work Corruption of Blood, or Forfeiture except during the Life of the Person attainted.

——United States Constitution, Article III, Section 3

Contents

INTRODUCTION

Another story has just broken—a plea for Russia to hack someone's e-mails, a meeting at the Trump Tower with a suspected Russian agent, or an announcement by the president of the United States that a hated political enemy has committed treason. In my office at the UC Davis School of Law in California, I know what will come next. The phone rings, and suddenly I am back in the world of Washington, where I used to practice law. On the line is a reporter with the inevitable question: "Is it really treason?"

As recently as early 2016, I rarely received calls like this. As a professor of American constitutional law and legal history, I regularly answer questions for the media about legal issues. But for the most part, those calls tended to focus on constitutional law more generally and on other subjects I have written about, such as the Second Amendment or the arcane law governing baby names. Few people were interested in one of my primary fields of research—the American law of treason.

Times have changed—and dramatically so. Treason, for lack of a better word, is now "hot" again. Ever since Donald Trump publicly encouraged Russia to hack the

DNC's e-mails, allegations of treason have hovered over Trump and his campaign, pushing the issue into a bright national spotlight. With each new sordid revelation, the stench of perceived disloyalty grows stronger. For many on the left, the notion that Donald Trump is a traitor isn't just a suspicion, it's an established fact.

Trump, too, is convinced that widespread treason is occurring, although he sees different culprits. By June 2019, he had made at least twenty-four separate accusations of treason, far more than any other modern president.[1] He has claimed, for example, that an FBI agent's support for Hillary Clinton amounted to "treason."[2] He suggested that Democratic members of Congress who failed to applaud during his State of the Union address were "un-American" and "treasonous."[3] When an anonymous member of his administration published a critical editorial in the *New York Times*, Trump tweeted, "TREASON?" He suggested that Democrats who opposed his border policies were "TREASONOUS."[4] And, when pressed by a reporter, he specifically accused former FBI director James Comey and assistant director Andrew McCabe of committing treason by investigating his campaign.[5] More recently, Trump stated that the Mueller investigation "was treason" and that the *New York Times* committed treason by publishing a story stating that the U.S. was increasing its cyberattacks on Russia.[6] Perhaps most notoriously, when Adam Schiff, chair of the House Intelligence Committee, criticized Trump's phone call with Ukraine's president, Trump tweeted, "Arrest for Treason?"[7]

But it's not just Trump. If you look carefully, you can

find accusations of treason everywhere; nearly every prominent politician has been accused of treason at some point, often in hysterical and breathless prose. From some of the less reputable corners of the internet, we learn, "JUST IN: Chuck Schumer Just Got The WORST NEWS EVER!—Treason Charges Probable . . ."[8] and "BREAKING: Trump U.S. District Attorney to Pursue TREASON Charges Against Barack Obama!"[9] A MoveOn.org petition demanding a treason trial of Mitch McConnell has attracted over 2,100 signatures. The petition claims that McConnell is "purposefully hurting the American economy to benefit his Chinese father-in-law's businesses and industries. That is treason."[10] A Change.org petition demands "a thorough investigation by the FBI, into the practices of the DNC, to seek an indictment against Debbie Wasserman Schultz, and her co-conspirators, to bring them to justice for TREASON, against the American People."[11] The charges extend even into the worlds of Hollywood and professional sports. Actor Jon Voight recently accused Shia LaBeouf and Miley Cyrus of "teaching treason" by protesting Donald Trump.[12] And when Colin Kaepernick refused to stand for the national anthem, he was denounced as a "traitor" by NFL officials.[13]

What are we to make of this profusion of treason claims? Some of them are mere rhetorical hyperbole, a generic term for some perceived disloyalty. In casual conversation, for example, one might use the term "traitor" to describe a cheating spouse or a business partner hired away by a competitor. No one would interpret such a claim as referring to criminal activity.

Treason, however, also has a distinct legal meaning. Each nation defines treason differently, but the core concept is betrayal of one's country. In England and America, the law historically viewed treason as the most horrific crime a person could commit. Judges routinely described it as worse than murder, and the sentences imposed for treason bore this out. Whereas murderers were merely hanged, convicted traitors in England received a far more brutal and elaborate punishment. The culprit was drawn to the gallows behind a cart, and then partially hanged by the neck. While he was still alive, his entrails were taken out and burned in front of him, his genitals were cut off, and, finally, he was decapitated. His body was sliced into four pieces, which were then placed on stakes alongside the head in highly visible locations. It was believed, probably correctly, that this procedure would have a significant deterrent effect on all who witnessed it.[14]

Many of the current allegations about treason, though, are not merely rhetoric, but sincere (although often incorrect) assertions that a person has committed a criminal offense. Such claims are made to encourage a prosecution, possibly leading to an execution or at least to a lengthy sentence of imprisonment. These allegations should not be tossed around lightly. To accuse someone of treason is to accuse him or her of the most significant offense known to American law.

But what exactly is treason? The answer would appear to be simple—the crime is specifically defined in the

"Treason Clause" of Article III of the U.S. Constitution, which states, "Treason against the United States, shall consist only in levying War against them, or in adhering to their Enemies, giving them Aid and Comfort." The language is clear and seemingly nontechnical. Why would a reporter, or anyone else, need to turn to an expert?

In reality, the Treason Clause turns out to be constitutional quicksand. In a 1945 decision, the United States Supreme Court warned that the Treason Clause's "superficial appearance of clarity and simplicity . . . proves illusory when it is put to practical application. There are few subjects on which the temptation to utter abstract interpretive generalizations is greater or on which they are more to be distrusted. The little clause is packed with controversy and difficulty."[15]

Supreme Court justices are not usually so candid about the difficulty of their cases. But "controversy and difficulty" is an entirely appropriate summary of American treason law, a field in which seemingly obvious intuitions are often wildly off the mark. The body of law surrounding treason is complex, contested, and often rooted in even more obscure strands of English law. As a result, there is usually no simple answer available on the internet or anywhere else.[16]

Controversy, difficulty, and complexity, however, are not desirable qualities in a nation's criminal law, which is supposed to provide clear notice as to what conduct is prohibited and what is not. The allegations about Donald Trump have greatly increased public curiosity about treason, but it is more difficult than it should be for interested citizens to find reliable information about the offense.

Increasingly shrill accusations of treason on all sides of the political spectrum have done little to advance public understanding; indeed, they tend to muddy the issue far more than to clarify it. What is needed is a reliable overview of the American law of treason that everyone can understand.

On Treason has two broad goals. First, this book seeks to explain, in language clearly intelligible to nonlawyers, the core principles of American treason law, including many areas that are not widely understood. My intent is to arm the reader with the tools to identify what counts as treason and what does not in the vast majority of cases. Sometimes the question can be genuinely hard, because there are issues that haven't been squarely resolved by courts, or because modern developments have challenged the factual assumptions underlying certain doctrines. In these cases, I have tried to lay out the arguments on both sides, recognizing that courts might resolve the issue either way. The appendix allows you to test your knowledge by applying the law to a variety of factual situations in the form of bar exam–style questions.[17]

Second, the book relates the stories of significant treason cases in American history. Although treason trials are now a rarity, they have played an important role in our country's development. Our very existence as an independent nation was formed in an act of treason against Great Britain. Our greatest national crisis, the Civil War, was triggered by the decision of Southern states to traitorously wage war against the United States. The stories of Benedict Arnold, Aaron Burr, Jefferson Davis, and others are fascinating, not just because of their colorful details, but because they illuminate fundamental aspects of our national identity.

Although all law is deeply rooted in history, treason law bears an especially distinctive historical imprint. The law of treason cannot be understood without knowledge of the historical circumstances that gave rise to the doctrine, and the history of particular treason trials cannot be understood without knowledge of the legal doctrine that governed them. This book accordingly interweaves chapters focused primarily on legal doctrine with chapters exploring particular cases. But the historical chapters contain plenty of law, and the legal chapters contain plenty of history.

We can begin the story in the sweltering Assembly Room of Independence Hall in Philadelphia in the summer of 1787, where the delegates to the Constitutional Convention drafted the Treason Clause of the United States Constitution. The words were written in English and in many respects appeared quite modern. But the key phrases were actually over four hundred years old, echoing the words of an English statute, originally written in French, to solve a dispute about the inheritance of land.

So let's open the doors to the Assembly Room and see how the drafters made the fateful decision to constitutionalize American treason law, a decision that still governs the fates and fortunes of the disloyal over two hundred and thirty years later.

1

The English Origins of American Treason Law and the Adoption of the Constitution's Treason Clause

In reality, we wouldn't be allowed to open the doors to the Constitutional Convention. The Convention met in secret, fearful that any publicizing of its deliberations would risk undermining the final product. So if we sneaked into the room in late August 1787, what would we find? Hot, sweaty, grumpy men who had been deliberating for several months and were eager to wrap it up and head home. Philadelphia in August is usually hideous, and it was especially hideous without air-conditioning, in uncomfortable clothing, and in a room with the windows and doors tightly sealed up. To a modern nose, the aroma would probably not have been particularly appealing.

But the delegates were doing something extraordinary

on that August day. They were writing into the nation's proposed constitution a definition of treason. No state constitution had contained any such provision. But here, enshrined in the "supreme law of the land," would be a binding definition of treason that Congress and presidents could not alter. "Treason against the United States," the delegates wrote, "shall consist only in levying War against them, or in adhering to their Enemies, giving them Aid and Comfort." It is the only crime specifically defined in the Constitution.

Although defining treason in a national constitution was a new idea, the phrases the delegates used were not pulled out of thin air. Every lawyer at the Convention, and probably most nonlawyers as well, would have understood the significance of the terms employed in the definition. They were technical legal terms, rooted in an English statute that was over four hundred years old.

In 1351, the English Parliament enacted the Statute of Treasons.[1] Like all English statutes at the time, it was written in French. Ever since the Norman Conquest of 1066, French was the formal language of English government. The statute limited the crime of treason to seven basic offenses. Roughly translated, they are (1) compassing or imagining the death of the king, the queen, or their eldest son and heir; (2) violating the wife of the king, the king's eldest unmarried daughter, or the wife of the king's eldest son; (3) levying war against the king in his realm; (4) adhering to the king's enemies in his realm, giving them aid and comfort in the realm, or elsewhere; (5) counterfeiting; (6) killing the chancellor, the treasurer, or the king's justices; and (7) the murder of a master by a servant, a husband by a wife, or a prelate by a cleric. The seventh category would later come to be called "petty treason" to distinguish it from the others, which constituted "high treason."

The framers used this statute as the starting point for their definition of treason. It was easy to see that many of the offenses in the English statute would be inappropriate in the new republic of the United States. Accordingly, the Convention dropped the provisions about compassing the king's death. Not only was there no king in America, but this provision had generated some of the most egregious abuses under English law. Sleeping with the king's wife was easily dispensed with. Counterfeiting was obviously a serious crime, but it no longer seemed like high treason, so the Convention empowered Congress to punish counterfeiting as a separate offense. Similarly, the Convention dropped the provisions about killing high government officials—presumably murder laws would be sufficient to deal with the problem. And there was no suggestion that "petty treason" had any business being in the Constitution. What was left was levying war against the king in his realm, which the framers changed to "levying war against [the United States]," and adhering to the king's enemies in his realm or elsewhere, which the framers changed to "adhering to their enemies, giving them aid and comfort." Thus our Constitution contains language, roughly verbatim, from an English statute that is now over six hundred and fifty years old.

Why did the English Parliament feel a need to limit the scope of treason in 1351? As historian J. G. Bellamy has pointed out, the statute was "a direct result of the royal judges trying to extend the common law of treason."[2] To some extent, Parliament was concerned about protecting English subjects from abusive treason prosecutions. But money was probably an even more significant factor. In 1351, England was still a feudal society, in which almost all wealth was held in the form of land.[3] Under the feudal system, "tenants" held interests in land from their "lords," and these interests were subject to a variety of complicated rules, including restrictions on inheritance. If a tenant died without an heir, the land returned to the lord's control, and he could now grant it to someone else (for a fee, of course). A felony conviction had the same effect—the convicted felon's lands would be returned to his lord. In both of these circumstances, death without heir and felony conviction, the land was said to have "escheated" to the lord.

But there was an important exception to the escheat rule. If the tenant was convicted of treason, the land reverted directly to the king, and the lord received nothing. Accordingly, powerful landholders had a strong interest in seeing the crime of treason narrowly defined. Every treason conviction was effectively a hit to their pocketbooks. The petitions to narrow the law of treason all emphasized the loss of the escheats as a primary justification.[4] So the Parliament of 1351, composed largely of wealthy landholders, adopted the Statute of Treasons in large part to shore up its own financial interests.

As the feudal system gradually disintegrated, this justification for the law was largely forgotten, and the Statute of Treasons became celebrated as a great gift from Parliament to the people. In the early seventeenth century, for example, the famous jurist Sir Edward Coke wrote that the Parliament that enacted the statute "was called Benedictum Parliamentum [Blessed Parliament], as it well deserved." Coke argued that the only English legislation more honored than the Statute of Treasons was the Magna Carta.[5]

This view was shared by the members of the Constitutional Convention. Pennsylvania delegate James Wilson, a primary architect of the Treason Clause, was later appointed to the Supreme Court by President George Washington. In a celebrated series of law lectures delivered while he was a justice, Wilson explicitly linked the Treason Clause to the English Statute of Treasons. Wilson argued that the Constitution's definition of treason was deliberately "transcribed from a part of the statute of Edward the third" so that its language would be "recommended by the mature experience, and ascertained by the legal interpretation, of numerous revolving centuries." Wilson added, "This statute has been in England, except during times remarkably tyrannical or turbulent, the governing rule with regard to treasons ever since. Like a rock, strong by nature, and fortified, as successive occasions required, by the able and honest assistance of art, it has been impregnable by all the rude and boisterous assaults, which have been made upon it, at different quarters, by ministers and judges; and as an object of national security, as well as of national pride, it may be well styled the legal Gibraltar of England."[6]

Three significant legal results flow directly from Article III's definition of treason and its explicit use of terminology from the English Statute of Treasons. First, as the word "or" in the clause makes clear, there are two distinct forms of treason: (1) levying war against the United States; and (2) adhering to their enemies, giving them aid and comfort. Each was treated as a completely distinct offense under English law, and each had its own particular definition. American law has followed this practice and has treated the offenses as entirely separate. One can levy war against the United States, for example, without adhering to our enemies, just as one can provide aid and comfort to our enemies without levying war against the United States (sending money to the enemy is an obvious example).

Second, because the Treason Clause requires that treason consists *only* of levying war or adhering to enemies, the law of treason cannot be applied to ordinary political disputes or disagreements about governmental policy. Harshly criticizing the government, for example, can never be the basis of a treason prosecution. As Chief Justice John Marshall explained in 1807, treason is the "most atrocious offense which can be committed against the political body, so it is the charge which is most capable of being employed as the instrument of those malignant and vindictive passions which may rage in the bosoms of contending parties struggling for power."[7] A year later, Justice Henry Brockholst Livingston explained that the definition of treason was made part of the "great fundamental law," so that it would not be "changed on a sudden emergency, so as to gratify the vengeance or promote the views of aspiring or designing men."[8] Under the Constitution, treason cannot be expanded at the whims of persons in power to oppress political opponents.

Third, the definition of treason cannot be broader in the United States than it was in England at the time of the adoption of the Constitution. "Levying war" and "adhering to enemies" were technical terms of English law that had a precise and well-understood meaning. American courts have considered arguments that American treason law is *narrower* than its English predecessor. As we will see, the meaning of "levying war," for example, is probably narrower under modern American law than it was under English law in 1787. But no court has interpreted these terms as *broader* than they were understood in English law (say, by construing "adhering to enemies" in a more expansive fashion). Indeed, any such argument would falter on the Treason Clause's emphatic use of the word "only." If the definition of treason could be broadened as well as narrowed, the term "only" would lose any operative meaning, thus entirely defeating the restrictive purposes of the Treason Clause.

Although the definition of treason is the most well-known aspect of the Treason Clause, the drafters included several other significant provisions governing trials and punishments. The Convention added a requirement stating that "No Person shall be convicted of Treason unless on the Testimony of two Witnesses to the same overt Act, or on Confession in open Court." English law had long required proof of an overt act and the testimony of two witnesses in treason cases. But those witnesses could testify to different overt acts. The Constitution significantly tightened this requirement by requiring two witnesses to the *same* overt act. No other crime in America is subject to this rigid evidentiary requirement. Moreover, English law had allowed convictions based solely on out-of-court confessions, if two witnesses testified to the confession.[9] Such convictions are impermissible under the Treason Clause, which requires that confessions be made in open court.[10]

The Treason Clause also provides that "The Congress shall have Power to declare the Punishment of Treason." Under English law, as noted in the Introduction, the punishment for treason was unbelievably horrific. This punishment had been occasionally ordered during the American Revolution, but it was never actually carried out. Every convicted traitor was simply hanged.[11] The Constitution doesn't formally mandate the death penalty for treason, instead granting discretion to Congress to determine the form of the punishment. Although the early Congresses set the penalty at death (presumably by hanging), current law provides courts with greater flexibility. Death is still a permissible sentence, but it can be as low as five years in prison coupled with a $10,000 fine.[12]

The Treason Clause ends by stating, "no Attainder of Treason shall work Corruption of Blood, or Forfeiture except during the Life of the Person attainted." This terminology is so arcane that it would mystify even most well-trained lawyers of today. So here's a rough translation into modern terms: under English law, an "attainder of treason" was a finding that a person was guilty of treason. This could happen in one of two ways: (1) conviction by a jury; or (2) a bill of attainder enacted in Parliament that would declare a person guilty without a trial. Either form of attainder carried two legal consequences (in addition to death): forfeiture and corruption of blood.

Forfeiture meant that the attainted person forfeited his entire estate to the Crown, meaning, of course, that his heirs would never inherit his property. "Corruption of blood" was even more pernicious. Under this doctrine, the person attainted was deemed to have never legally existed. His blood had been "corrupted," and no person could inherit by descent from his bloodline. To take a simple example, suppose the Earl of Bedford had one son, James, and James, in turn, had one son, Charles. If James died before his father, his son Charles would inherit the Earldom of Bedford and all of his grandfather's property upon the Earl of Bedford's death. But if James had been convicted and executed for treason, Charles would lose all inheritance rights against his grandfather's estate. His claim is based on his status as James's son, but, for legal purposes, James never existed. The earl's lands and title will pass to his closest male relative, excluding Charles. These consequences were highly significant, especially in a society like England's, where, until very recently, most wealth was held in the form of land.

The drafters of the American Constitution viewed these punishments for treason with abhorrence. In effect, they punished children for the sins of their fathers, punishing the innocent along with the guilty. Accordingly, the Treason Clause prohibits corruption of blood—for inheritance purposes, a convicted traitor is treated the same as anyone else. Similarly, any forfeiture of property will last only as long as the traitor is alive. After that, the property will return to his heirs. And by prohibiting bills of attainder (in a separate provision of the Constitution), the drafters ensured that treason convictions would only be obtained through jury trials.

Finally, it is worth noting a significant limitation of the Treason Clause—it governs only a small subset of a wide range of disloyal behavior. Under the Treason Clause, the government is severely restricted with respect to what can be punished as treason. But the Clause does not prevent the government from criminalizing all kinds of other disloyal behavior as offenses distinct from treason.[13] To take one example, it is not treason to spy for a country that is a friendly ally of the United States. But Congress can still punish this disloyalty as espionage. As early as 1807, the United States Supreme Court warned that the "crime of treason should not be extended by construction to doubtful cases," because Congress was always free to create separate punishments for "crimes not clearly within the constitutional definition."[14] A century later, a federal appellate court noted that "it has never been doubted that Congress may punish . . . acts which are of a seditious nature and tend toward treason, but which are not of the direct character . . . which would meet the constitutional test and make them treason."[15] Indeed, these offenses can even carry the death penalty, as is the case with espionage.

But if one can be executed for other forms of disloyalty does it really matter that the Constitution imposes such severe restrictions on treason? Under English law, the distinction between treason and other crimes made sense, because the punishments were different, most notably in the form of execution. But under American law there is little difference between being executed for treason and being executed for some other crime of disloyalty, such as espionage (like the Rosenbergs). So does the Treason Clause continue to serve any useful purpose?

I think that it does. As legal scholar James Willard Hurst pointed out, there is a "peculiar intimidation and stigma carried by the mere accusation of treason."[16] Moreover, as the furor over Donald Trump has indicated, many Americans have a powerful desire to define conduct that they find reprehensively disloyal as treason. For some people, it is not enough that Trump's and his associates' actions may well violate a host of other federal criminal laws—they want him and them to go down for treason, and nothing less. This very intensity of feeling in times of political ferment may itself be the best evidence of the framers' wisdom in carefully defining the crime.

2

Benedict Arnold: Founding Traitor

When the military men arrived, the young woman appeared completely out of her senses, shrieking and crying at the top of her lungs. Peggy Shippen, a glamorous Philadelphia socialite, had married a prominent American general nineteen years her senior, and was now living in a house near the fort of West Point, New York. Hours earlier, her husband had disappeared down the Hudson River, fleeing to the British. Now the house was swarming with American officers, including George Washington and Alexander Hamilton, who found Shippen utterly enchanting and gallantly sought to console her. They believed every word she uttered, convinced that she had been the innocent victim of a worthless husband. Hamilton wrote to his fiancée that "It was the most affecting scene I ever was witness to. . . . All the sweetness of beauty, all the loveliness of innocence, all the tenderness of a wife and all the fondness of a mother showed themselves in her appearance and conduct."[1]

But the shrieks and cries were all an act, one of the finest bits of theatrical performance in the American Revolution—a mad scene to rival any on the London stage. Peggy Shippen had just played Washington and Hamilton for dupes. Far from being in shock, she had been working closely with her husband every step of the way for nearly a year and a half.[2] According to a later account, when Shippen was finally clear of the scene, she admitted that she was "heartily tired of the theatrics she was exhibiting."[3] History has largely remembered her by her maiden name, Peggy (short for "Margaret") Shippen, but she was also known by another name—Mrs. Benedict Arnold.

Over two hundred and thirty years after his attempted betrayal of West Point, Benedict Arnold remains the quintessential American traitor, his name synonymous with treason itself. Indeed, his dark deeds reverberate to this very day in the naming patterns of children. Benedict is not an uncommon name in Great Britain (think of the actor Benedict Cumberbatch). In 1999, it was the 165th most popular boy name in England and Wales. By 2015, it had fallen to 341st most popular, but still comfortably within the top 1,000.[4] By contrast (according to records going back to 1900), Benedict peaked in popularity in the United States in 1914 as the 447th most popular boy name. It has not been in the top 1,000 names since 1968.[5] In the United States, the name "Benedict" can hardly be spoken without calling to mind the treacherous Benedict Arnold.

For most Americans, Benedict Arnold is an almost mythical character, a figure out of a melodrama, the very personification of evil. But the real story of Benedict Arnold is even more fascinating than the myth, and presents many mind-boggling twists of fate.

Born in 1741 in Connecticut, Arnold had been a New Haven shopkeeper and a captain of merchant vessels plying the trade between New England, the Caribbean, and Canada. When the news of the Battle of Lexington reached New Haven, Arnold immediately led a group of men to defend his country against the British assault. He was a leader in the successful attack on Fort Ticonderoga and won renown for his valiant service during the siege of Quebec in the fall of 1775. In 1776, he performed heroically as a naval commander at the Battle of Valcour Island on Lake Champlain. In 1777, he was critical to the American victory at the Battle of Saratoga, which led to the all-important alliance with France. Arnold's horse was killed beneath him, and bullets shattered his left leg (which he had previously wounded at Quebec). George Washington viewed Arnold as perhaps his best fighting general, and Arnold's fame extended to Great Britain and even into Europe more broadly.[6]

An Arnold who had died in 1777 would likely have numerous statues in his honor, paintings commemorating his exploits, a portrait in the United States Capitol or the White House, and possibly even schools and universities named after him. There could easily be a Benedict Arnold

College at Yale University, to commemorate one of New Haven's most distinguished citizens. Arnold would be in the pantheon of immortal American heroes, one of the country's indisputably great military leaders and a man indispensable to the success of the American Revolution.

But Benedict Arnold survived the Battle of Saratoga, and instead went on to become the most reviled man in the nation's history. In May 1779, Arnold secretly offered his services to the British, who instructed him to remain on the American side until they could determine the most effective way to use him.

Why would a man so seemingly committed to the American cause even consider switching sides? A complex set of factors played into Arnold's decision. When his treason was revealed, outraged Americans believed that he had turned his coat solely for financial gain. And money was clearly on Arnold's mind. In his negotiations with the British, he put considerable effort into ensuring that he would be handsomely rewarded for his efforts. But it wasn't just about money. Arnold had feuded repeatedly with his fellow generals and had a stormy relationship with the Continental Congress, which he felt had been insufficiently appreciative of his military service. During his tenure in Philadelphia, following the city's recapture from the British in 1778, he had alienated Pennsylvania's civilian leadership, including Joseph Reed, who accused Arnold of numerous acts of corruption.

Arnold's April 1779 marriage to Peggy Shippen also

played a role. Shippen had strong Loyalist sympathies, and she had interacted regularly with British officers during the city's occupation. Although it is not clear that she originated the idea of Arnold's betrayal, she did everything she could to facilitate it. Historian Stephen Brumwell also points to Arnold's growing dissatisfaction with the war and an apparent belief that Americans would be better off if the war were over, even if it meant returning to some form of limited British control. And Arnold was repelled by the American alliance with France, a Catholic country that he (along with most British-Americans) had long disdained.[7]

After months of secret letters to enemy lines, the details of the British plan to employ Arnold for maximum effect began to emerge in the summer of 1780. Arnold would secure command of the key fort of West Point, which was located at a pivotal site on the Hudson River. The British had occupied New York City since 1776, but had failed to secure control of the Hudson. The fall of West Point would give Britain mastery of the entire river, separating the New England colonies from the rest of the United States, cutting critical American supply lines, and possibly hastening the end of the war in Britain's favor.

In August 1780, Arnold took over the command of West Point, and it looked as if his scheme was going to succeed. Arnold ordered American troops to perform a variety of tasks away from the fort, such as cutting firewood, defending a more remote fort downriver, and escorting prisoners to Washington's camp; he also sold off many of the fort's provisions. With diminished manpower and supplies, the fort would be even more vulnerable to a British attack.[8] In another stroke of luck for Arnold, George Washington turned out to be in the vicinity, raising the tantalizing possibility that the British might capture both West Point and the American commander in chief.

Arnold's treason was on the verge of success, until another twist of fate intervened. Major John André, Arnold's primary British contact, took an unplanned and circuitous route back to British lines after a meeting with Arnold near West Point. On the east side of the Hudson River, disguised in civilian clothes, he was stopped by three New York militiamen who asked him what party he belonged to. André replied, "The lower," referring to British-occupied New York. The militiamen then pretended to be British supporters as well, at which point André revealed himself to be a British officer. After announcing their true identities, the militiamen strip-searched André and discovered incriminating documents hidden in his boots. The game was up, and the damning details were sent on to American officials.[9] Arnold learned of the discovery just shortly before General Washington did, and fled to the British in the nick of the time. Only Arnold's wife remained at his house when Washington arrived. For General Nathanael Greene, the plot's discovery was nothing short of a miracle. In his widely circulated general orders, he noted, "The providential train of circumstances which led to it affords the most convincing proof that the Liberties of America are the object of divine Protection."[10]

But what if those militiamen had been slightly less attentive? If the British had captured West Point, they would have achieved a key strategic victory that could have altered the course of the entire war. It is even conceivable that the War for Independence could have been lost and the colonies returned to British control. Three militiamen may well have held the nation's fate in their hands.

Arnold's escape meant that Americans would be deprived of the satisfaction of seeing him swinging at the end of a rope. Had he been captured, he would have been subject to a trial before a court-martial, and would almost certainly have been hanged. But the states took what limited action they could. Pennsylvania, where Arnold had most recently lived, attainted Arnold as a traitor. Under Pennsylvania's peculiar 1776 constitution, executive authority was located in a committee, called the Supreme Executive Council, rather than a governor. A 1777 state law had authorized the Council to issue proclamations of attainder. Under this procedure, persons would be "proclaimed" by the Council as traitors, and if they failed to show up for trial within a specified period of time, they would be deemed "attainted," that is, deemed to be legally convicted of treason. Their real estate and personal property could be seized for the benefit of the state, and if they were captured, they could be executed without a trial. Arnold remained an attainted traitor in Pennsylvania until his death, the closest he came to legal punishment.[11] Similarly, in Connecticut, Arnold's house in New Haven was deemed forfeited to the state and sold (it was later occupied by the dictionary writer Noah Webster).[12]

For Arnold, the war continued as before, just with a British uniform. He commanded a regiment of Loyalists, and even led a raid against his home state of Connecticut.[13] But when the war ended, he left for Britain, never to return to the United States.

Peggy Shippen, Arnold's wife, had left West Point soon after the treason was discovered, and returned to her father's house in Philadelphia. Her vivid theatrics had ensured that she would initially be seen as an innocent victim of Arnold's scheming. But a month later, Pennsylvania's Supreme Executive Council banished her from the state, and she rejoined her husband in New York.[14]

As more and more documents came to light in the twentieth century, Peggy's deep involvement in the plot has become impossible to deny. She fully supported Arnold's treason, had nurtured it for well over a year, and had been aware of his plans to surrender West Point. Indeed, it is likely that if she had strongly encouraged Arnold to retain his American loyalty, he might have refrained from turning to the British. She, too, was a traitor, probably the most significant female traitor in American history. And she was well rewarded by the British, receiving a significant pension from King George III for what General Henry Clinton described as "her services, which were meritorious."[15] In fairness, we should probably refer to Benedict and Peggy Arnold together in the same way that we refer to Julius and Ethel Rosenberg. It was "the Arnolds" who were traitors, Peggy as much as Benedict.

Benedict Arnold was hardly the only American to side with the British during the American Revolution. Thousands of Americans, ranging from prominent to obscure, retained their loyalty to the British government. William Franklin, the nonmarital son of Benjamin Franklin, for example, was a consistent supporter of British policies. Many men who had held high office in colonial America initially supported resistance efforts, but found themselves unable to support American independence. Large numbers fled to the protection of the British army and ultimately to Britain itself or to other British colonies.

When the war was over, however, a significant reconciliation occurred. As time passed, older passions cooled, and the Loyalist refugees who wished to return made their way back to America, where they were largely accepted as fellow citizens.[16] Even Peggy Shippen spent five months in Philadelphia visiting her father in 1789–1790.[17] After a long, bitter civil war, people were willing to forgive old faults and let bygones be bygones.

Except for Benedict Arnold. He remained the arch-American traitor, the one person who would never be allowed back. If he had dared to set foot in America, he would have been immediately arrested for treason and almost certainly executed. What made Arnold so distinctive?

First, Arnold was a very high-ranking member of the Continental Army. Hardly any officers, much less generals, deserted to the British. High-ranking civilians who fled to the British were far less capable of inflicting real harm. Arnold, with access to the nation's most vital military secrets, could inflict far more damage to the American cause than almost anyone else. The potential harm of Arnold's treason was incalculable, and Americans responded with raging fury and disbelief. As legal scholar Robert Ferguson pointed out, "No other episode of the Revolutionary War produced such a broad series of intense emotional responses among wartime participants as this one."[18]

Second, most of the other well-known men who sided with the British did so relatively early on in the conflict. Once it was clear that a war was ongoing and that independence was the aim, people with principled reasons to retain their loyalty did so unmistakably. Arnold, by contrast, did so very late in the war. The plot was revealed in September 1780, over five and a half years since fighting had broken out at Lexington. For almost the entire war, Arnold had been a seemingly devoted member of the American side. To desert so late in the game suggested that motives other than honest disagreement were at play.

Third, and related to the prior point, Arnold was widely perceived as having betrayed the United States solely for monetary gain. This rendered his crime nearly incomprehensibly evil. Arnold was not simply a fellow citizen with a fundamental disagreement about politics—he was Satan himself. According to American general Nathanael Greene, "Never since the fall of Lucifer has a fall equaled his."[19]

In the end, Arnold's treason accomplished nothing. A little over a year later, American and French forces won a significant victory at Yorktown, and in 1783, Britain finally recognized American independence. Other than seven years spent in New Brunswick, Arnold lived the rest of his life in England, where he died in 1801, leaving a surprising provision in his will for a fourteen-year-old boy in Canada, possibly a nonmarital child.[20] Peggy survived him by three years, dying in 1804 of uterine cancer at the age of forty-four.[21]

The only American monuments to Benedict Arnold are at the Saratoga Battlefield, where he performed his most heroic acts of military valor. But the commemoration, unsurprisingly, is muted. A large obelisk, erected between 1877 and 1882, features statues of prominent American commanders on three sides of the exterior: Horatio Gates, Philip Schuyler, and Daniel Morgan. On the fourth side is a blank space, where a statue of Arnold would normally have been included.[22] Inside the monument are plaques depicting significant events. The thirteenth plaque portrays the wounding of General Arnold.[23] On the location of his injury, a small monument, erected in 1887, states, "In memory of the 'most brilliant soldier' of the Continental army, who was desperately wounded on this spot . . . 7th October 1777, winning for his countrymen the Decisive Battle of the American Revolution."[24] There is no mention of Arnold's name, just a depiction of an officer's left-footed boot—an entirely fitting memorial. When Arnold was serving on the British side, he asked an American prisoner what the Americans would do to him if he were captured. The prisoner replied, "They would first cut off that lame leg, which was wounded in the cause of freedom and virtue, and bury it with the honors of war, and afterwards hang the remainder of your body in gibbets."[25]

Symbolically, this is precisely how Arnold continues to be remembered. The "Burning of Benedict Arnold Festival" in New London, Connecticut, attracts hundreds of people each year. Based on an earlier tradition that died out during the Civil War, a theater company publicly burns Benedict Arnold in effigy. But first, the effigy's leg is removed and pardoned, before the rest is consigned to the flames.[26]

3

What Is "Levying War Against the United States"?

Under Article III, it is treason to levy war against the United States, but what does this actually mean? Consider four possible scenarios: (1) a large army is assembled, which marches on Washington, DC, with the intent to overthrow the government; it is defeated outside the city in a large battle; (2) a man recently released from federal prison following a money laundering conviction is convinced that the local FBI office had framed him; armed with automatic weapons, he and his wife burst into the FBI office and begin firing, killing fifteen people; (3) upset about federal environmental regulation, twelve ranchers seize a federal park building and hold it by armed force, requiring federal officers to storm the building in order to remove them; (4) a woman opposed to American military policy plants a dirty bomb in the Pentagon, seeking to disable the United States military. The bomb explodes, killing one hundred employees and rendering the Pentagon unusable for at least a year. Have any of these people committed treason by levying war against the United States?

The answers are (1) yes; (2) no; (3) probably not; and (4) maybe. The first one is easy—it is the quintessential case of levying war against the United States, a scenario that only really occurred during the American Civil War. The second one is also easy—the killers acted entirely out of private motives, with no intent to overthrow the government. They can be punished for murder, but not for treason. The third and fourth scenarios are more difficult, as they raise complicated questions about the meaning of levying war in the twenty-first century.

The drafters of Article III adopted the phrase "levying war against the United States" from the 1351 English Statute of Treasons, which had prohibited "levying war against the king in his realm." By the time the Constitution was adopted, English judges had been parsing this statute for over four hundred years.

The clearest cases under English law were armed insurrections that sought to dethrone or imprison the king or that sought to force him to alter his decisions or to remove members of his government.[1] But insurrections that didn't directly target the king could also amount to treason. If an armed insurrection sought to alter the established law, to change the state religion, or to free all the country's prisoners, for example, it would be deemed an act of levying war (sometimes referred to as "constructive" levying of war). As English jurist Michael Foster explained, such insurrections were nonetheless against the crown's royal dignity, because they used armed force, rather than peaceable measures, to effect political change.[2]

The key, however, was that the insurrectionists must be motivated by some broad public concern. If the insurrection was merely the result of some private quarrel, for example, it was not treason. So an armed march to rescue a particular prisoner from a prison would not be treason, but a march to release *all* prisoners would be. Similarly, forcible resistance to a particular tax collector would not be treason if, say, the resistors simply believed the collector had been improperly appointed to his job, but an insurrection to suppress *all* tax collection would be.

Moreover, a conspiracy to levy war was not a levying of war. Actual force had to be employed for an act of levying war to take place. (English courts, however, allowed conspiracies to levy war to be punished as acts of compassing the king's death.)

These broad principles of English law seem to have been accepted largely without question at the time of the Constitution's adoption. In 1807, in the Aaron Burr case, Chief Justice John Marshall noted that levying war is a "technical term. It is used in a very old statute of that country whose language is our language, and whose laws form the substratum of our laws. It is scarcely conceivable that the term was not employed by the framers of our constitution in the sense which had been affixed to it by those from whom we borrowed it."[3] In the late 1770s, Chief Justice Thomas McKean of Pennsylvania, a signer of the Declaration of Independence, followed the English authorities almost verbatim when delivering charges to grand juries.[4] Similarly, James Wilson, a member of the Constitutional Convention and a justice of the United States Supreme Court, closely followed Foster's definition of levying war in the early 1790s.[5]

Many of the English decisions on levying war continue to shape American treason law. For example, armed insurrections to overthrow the U.S. government are paradigm cases of levying war against the United States, analogous to raising an army to overthrow the king. And any person who assists with the military aspects of the insurrection is potentially guilty of treason. As Chief Justice John Marshall explained in 1807, "All those who perform the various and essential military parts of prosecuting the war . . . may with correctness and accuracy be said to levy war."[6]

In one significant respect, however, modern American treason law is probably narrower than the English precedents on levying of war. It is hard to make confident assertions, as the most significant judicial decisions are over two hundred years old, and the federal government has not indicted anyone within the United States for levying war since the nineteenth century. But it seems likely that insurrections seeking the repeal of particular laws, without any broader attempt to overthrow the United States government, will no longer be held to be treasonous.

The early American decisions initially followed English law quite closely on this point. In 1794, the Whiskey Rebellion erupted in western Pennsylvania out of opposition to the federal excise tax on whiskey.[7] Although the Whiskey Rebels had no intent to overthrow the federal government, they burned down the house of a federal tax collector, and thousands of armed men gathered in opposition to the law. The Washington administration indicted twenty men for treason, and Supreme Court Justice William Paterson, presiding over the trials, agreed that the rebellion constituted treason under English precedents. If the object of the insurrection, Paterson instructed the jury, "was to suppress the excise offices, and to prevent the execution of an act of Congress, by force and intimidation," then the Whiskey Rebels had committed high treason by levying war against the United States.[8]

In 1799, resistance to a federal property tax in eastern Pennsylvania led to the so-called Fries's Rebellion. A group of four hundred armed men, led by John Fries, compelled a federal marshal to release prisoners who had been arrested for protesting the tax. Like the Whiskey Rebels, the Fries Rebels did not seek to overthrow the government of the United States—they simply sought the repeal of a particular tax. The John Adams administration nonetheless prosecuted Fries and several others for levying war against the United States. Fries was tried and convicted twice (his first conviction was thrown out because of procedural irregularities). Supreme Court justices presiding at both trials agreed that the alleged conduct constituted high treason. Justice Samuel Chase, for example, concluded that "any such insurrection or rising to resist or prevent by force or violence, the execution of any statute of the United States . . . is a levying of war against the United States."[9] President Adams, however, later had a change of heart and pardoned Fries, concluding that his "crime did not amount to treason. [He] had been guilty of a high-handed riot and rescue, attended with circumstances hot, rash, violent, and dangerous, but all these did not amount to treason."[10]

But many early-nineteenth-century courts continued to cite the judicial decisions from the Whiskey and Fries's Rebellion cases as valid precedents. During the 1807 treason trial of former vice president Aaron Burr (see chapter 4), Chief Justice John Marshall charged a grand jury that the use of force "to coerce the repeal or adoption of a general law" amounted to treason by levying war.[11] In 1842, Justice Joseph Story (the author of a prominent treatise on constitutional law) agreed, charging a grand jury that levying war did not require "a direct and positive intention entirely to subvert or overthrow the government." It was also treason "by force to prevent the execution of any one or more general and public laws of the government, or to resist the exercise of any legitimate authority of the government in its sovereign capacity."[12]

But other nineteenth-century judges disagreed, and argued for a more narrow definition of levying of war. In 1808, for example, Justice Henry Brockholst Livingston stated that a levying of war required the "embodying of a military force, armed and arrayed in a warlike manner, for the purpose of forcibly subverting the government, dismembering the Union, or destroying the legislative functions of congress. These troops should be so armed, and so directed, as to leave no doubt that the United States, or their government, were the immediate object of their attack."[13]

In 1851, Justice Robert Grier, charging the jury in the Castner Hanway case (see chapter 6), noted that the insurrection must "be to effect something of a public nature, to overthrow the government, or to nullify some law of the United States, and totally to hinder its execution, or counsel its repeal." But Grier pointedly observed that many of the English cases relied on in the Whiskey Rebellion and Fries's Rebellion cases "have since been discredited, if not overruled in that country." The modern English view, Grier concluded, was that "levying war" should be "confined to insurrections and rebellions for the purpose of overthrowing the government by force and arms."[14]

The most recent examination of levying war occurred in 1922, following a prosecution under West Virginia state law of miners who had led an army of over eight thousand men in an attempt to end martial law in one West Virginia county and to release over one hundred prisoners held in custody (see chapter 5). The presiding judge complained that there were few decided precedents to guide him. "A great deal of law that we have on the subject of treason," he noted, "consists of the opinions of judges in their charges to grand juries, and of the opinions of textbook writers." Nonetheless, he concluded that a charge of levying war against the state "must be a design against the sovereignty of the State." There must be a purpose "by force and violence to commit some act or some acts which, if successful, will subvert the Government in whole or in part."[15]

So what is the current status of insurrections designed to prevent the operation of one particular federal law? Consider the third example at the beginning of this chapter—ranchers seizing federal land to protest environmental regulations, presumably with the intent of having those regulations rescinded. English law suggested that holding a fort against the king would be an act of levying war against him. Moreover, the Whiskey Rebellion and Fries's Rebellion cases suggest that the use of force to halt the enforcement of federal law would also be treasonous. And it is true that those cases have not been technically overruled. In his 1964 book *The American Law of Treason: Revolutionary and Early National Origins*, historian Bradley Chapin even went so far as to claim that those cases remain "good law to this day."[16] If Chapin was correct, the ranchers would have committed treason.

But the better view seems to be that of James Willard Hurst, who argued in 1971 that "this branch of the crime has become obsolete by nonuse and by critical reaction against it at the bar and in the courts."[17] As Hurst explained, "As long since in England, so in the United States since the Civil War, with one abortive exception, no effort seems to have been made to charge the crime of treason by levying war simply on the basis of a breach of the peace without a showing of a specific intent to overthrow the government."[18] No modern prosecutor is likely to bring a treason case against people who merely forcibly obstructed a federal law. In the extremely unlikely event that such a charge is brought, the probable result will be a ruling that such prosecutions are obsolete. Savvy prosecutors know better than to waste their time with treason charges that are unlikely to succeed and will instead charge the perpetrators with some other crime. It is therefore quite possible that the older doctrine from the Whiskey and Fries's Rebellion cases will technically remain on the books, even though functionally it is entirely a dead letter.

When the framers of the Treason Clause thought about levying war, they had a very specific image in mind—men gathering with guns, forming an army, and marching on the seat of government. But that scenario has been anachronistic for decades and is utterly implausible in the twenty-first century. If someone wants to decapitate our government, the tool of choice will not be an army, but some form of terrorist attack.

This modern form of levying war against the United States is exemplified by the events of September 11, 2001. Terrorists flew a hijacked plane into the Pentagon and had also targeted the White House and the Capitol. The purpose of the attack was to paralyze and incapacitate the United States government. Although the terrorists were not U.S. citizens, they were subject to U.S. treason law while here (see chapter 7). The existing precedents provide strong support for charging the terrorists with treason (of course, they all died in the attacks, so none ever went to court).

But September 11 involved nineteen men acting together. What if a lone individual perpetrates a terrorist attack against the federal government? Here's where things get tricky. The nineteenth-century decisions insisted that a lone individual was incapable of levying war by himself. In the treason trial of Aaron Burr, Chief Justice Marshall held, "War can only be levied by the employment of actual force. Troops must be embodied, men must be assembled, in order to levy war."[19] There must be "a warlike *assemblage*, carrying the appearance of force, and in a situation to practice hostility."[20] As Marshall put it, "Why is it that a single armed individual entering a boat, and sailing down the Ohio for the avowed purpose of attacking New Orleans, could not be said to levy war?" Because such a person "is apparently not in a condition to levy war."[21] Justice Joseph Story agreed, stating in an 1842 grand jury charge that levying of war required "an assembly of persons, met for the treasonable purpose" and the use of force to achieve it.[22]

The American precedents thus suggest that to levy war there must be both some use of force and an assemblage of men. But the reasoning was closely tied to the technology of the time. In the early nineteenth century, there was very little that a solitary individual could do to levy war against the United States. Force could not be wielded in the absence of an assemblage of men. At best, one individual might be able to fire a cannon at a government building, but such a person could be easily stopped and posed little significant danger to the state.

Twenty-first-century technology is very different. A lone individual can now potentially wield the power of thousands, if not millions, of eighteenth-century soldiers. One person with a suitcase nuke could obliterate an entire city. So how do we interpret levying war in a modern world?

There seem to be two possible options. One is to insist that the older decisions say what they say—treason by levying war requires an assemblage of men, period. If there is no assemblage, there is no treason. The other option is to conclude that the relevant legal requirement is the use of force. But what constitutes that force can change with technological developments. The early cases' insistence on an assemblage of men was simply a factual conclusion based on current realities. And factual conclusions are subject to revision. From a functional perspective, it seems silly to claim that we should be more worried by three men with guns than by one man with a suitcase nuke. Why should flying a plane into the Pentagon be an act of levying war against the United States if there are two terrorists in the cockpit, but not if there is only one?

This is not an easy issue, which is why the answer to the fourth scenario (an individual bombing the Pentagon) is maybe. It will eventually have to be addressed by any court considering the application of treason law to modern offenses. If courts insisted on an assemblage of men, then lone individuals could not, as a matter of law, levy war against the United States. And there would still remain difficult questions about what constitutes assemblage in the modern era. Would there be assemblage, for example, if people coordinated attacks over the internet or the telephone, but never actually met in person?

Sophisticated modern terrorists are increasingly likely to engage in cyberwarfare. If attacks are committed electronically, can they still be acts of levying war against the United States? The best way to approach this question is to consider the closest non-cyber analogy. The easiest cases are those that are largely indistinguishable from traditional acts of levying of war. When force is applied directly against the United States government for the purpose of incapacitating it, it shouldn't matter if the force used is electronic. All of the following would likely qualify: using a computer to hack into the Pentagon and launch a nuclear missile against Washington, DC; hacking into an airplane's computer and directing it to fly into the White House; and creating an electric surge that renders the nation's power grid unusable.

If cyberattacks are launched against nongovernmental institutions, however, the analogy to treason is less obvious. Suppose someone hacked Walmart, resulting in the destruction of its central computers and the loss of all of its data. The relevant nondigital analogy would seem to be burning down Walmart's headquarters. It's a crime, but it's not treason. Similarly, other types of cybercrimes don't easily analogize to treason either. For example, hacking into an organization (the Democratic National Committee, for example) to steal its documents seems most analogous to a burglary. As far as I'm aware, no one thought the Watergate burglars were guilty of treason. Spreading fake news on the internet seems most analogous to standing on a street corner handing out fraudulent pamphlets. Likewise, hacking a voting machine to change the results seems most analogous to ballot stuffing or ballot tampering. A crime has clearly been committed, but not the crime of levying war against the United States.

An additional difficult hurdle for prosecuting cyberterrorists is the constitutional requirement that any treason conviction be supported by the testimony of two witnesses to the same overt act, or by confession in open court. In many cases of cyberattacks, the two-witness requirement will be almost impossible to meet. By definition, such attacks are solitary and stealthy, and it is highly unlikely that two witnesses will have independently witnessed the perpetrator orchestrating the attack from his computer. Fortunately, almost all acts of cyberwarfare can be easily prosecuted as other crimes. Prudent prosecutors will likely pursue those charges rather than risking the unnecessary complexities of a treason prosecution.

It has been over a century since the last person was convicted of levying war against the United States (a case from the Philippines, see chapter 7), and it is unlikely that these cases will return to American courts any time soon. Although treason by aiding the enemy is easily subject to prosecution in the twenty-first century, the offense of levying war is arguably archaic, of interest only to historians.

Armed rebellions to overthrow the government are simply not going to happen.

But certain types of levying war may still occur, including terrorist acts and cyberwarfare. Prosecutors thinking about charges need to at least consider the possibility of treason, even if they ultimately decline to pursue it, due to problems with the "assemblage of men" issue or the two-witness requirement. The government, however, has many other charges in its toolbox to deal with serious acts of terrorism and cyberwarfare. Murder itself is sufficient to merit the death penalty or a life sentence, and crimes like arson can carry significant penalties. No one who has committed horrific acts against the United States is likely to escape punishment solely because of quirks in our treason law.

4

The Case of Aaron Burr

For much of the nineteenth century, Blennerhassett Island in the Ohio River was the most famous island in America. Passengers traveling downriver, between the modern states of West Virginia and Ohio, viewed the long, skinny island as one of the highlights of their journey.[1] For many it would have brought back memories of school days. Instruction in rhetoric almost always included the careful study and memorization of a florid speech by attorney William Wirt, which opened with a vivid depiction of Blennerhassett Island.[2]

The island's claim to fame, or infamy, arose on December 10, 1806. It was here, according to the federal government, that Aaron Burr, the former vice president of the United States, committed treason. It was a plausible charge, except for the inconvenient fact that Aaron Burr was nowhere near Blennerhassett Island on December 10, 1806, and was actually hundreds of miles away.

Everything about the treason trial of Aaron Burr was bizarre. Consider a modern analogy: In 2012, President Barack Obama drops Joe Biden as his running mate, and is reelected with a different vice president. In 2015, the Obama administration indicts Biden for treason (for trying to split the United States in half), and the trial is presided over by Chief Justice John Roberts, a bitter personal enemy (and second cousin, once removed) of President Obama. To spice it up even further, Chief Justice Roberts's mother-in-law is President Obama's first fiancée. The prime witness against Biden in the grand jury proceedings is General Colin Powell, who has been a secret agent of the Spanish government for years. And Biden has recently killed former treasury secretary Robert Rubin in a duel, and is under indictment for murder in New York and New Jersey.

Any screenwriter who proposed this plotline would be quickly laughed out of town, as it strains the credibility of even the most ridiculous Hollywood political thriller. Yet this is precisely what transpired during the second term of President Thomas Jefferson. The chief justice was John Marshall, Jefferson's second cousin, once removed, and the son-in-law of Jefferson's first fiancée. The witness was General James Wilkinson, the commanding general in the American West and governor of the Louisiana Territory, who for years had been a paid agent of the Spanish government.[3] And the former vice president, of course, was Aaron Burr, who had memorably killed former treasury secretary Alexander Hamilton in a duel.

Chief Justice Marshall later described the Burr treason trial as "the most unpleasant case which has ever been brought before a Judge in this or perhaps in any other country."[4] There is good reason to take him at his word. It remains the most extraordinary treason trial in United States history: a former vice president—the highest-ranking person ever charged with treason—ferociously prosecuted for a capital crime by the administration under which he had previously served.

Everything had gone wrong for Aaron Burr, a man who started out with enormous potential and promise. A talented lawyer, Burr was a graduate of Princeton and a distinguished veteran of the Continental Army (where he had served under Benedict Arnold). After one term as a United States senator from New York, Burr was tapped as Thomas Jefferson's running mate in the 1800 presidential election against incumbent President John Adams.

Under the original Constitution, the members of the Electoral College did not vote separately for president and vice president; they simply voted for two candidates. Whoever came in first became president, and whoever came in second became vice president. In a world without partisan politics, this system might have worked well. But it could lead to disastrous results if there were clearly distinct presidential and vice presidential candidates running together on the same partisan ticket.

In the 1790s, partisan politics emerged rapidly, requiring presidential electors to cast their votes carefully. Ideally, the presidential candidate should receive the most electoral votes; the vice presidential candidate should receive one fewer. In the 1800 election, Federalist electors did this properly, giving Charles Cotesworth Pinckney one fewer vote than John Adams. Republican electors, by contrast, did not, casting all of their votes for both Jefferson and Burr. The resulting tie in the Electoral College meant that the election would be decided by the House of Representatives. The lame-duck House was controlled by Federalists, and rumors began spreading that Federalists might select Burr as president in exchange for various political concessions. Burr initially declared that the clear intent was for Jefferson to be president, but he later muddied the waters by stating that he would accept the presidency if he was selected by the House.[5] After thirty-six failed ballots, Jefferson finally secured a House majority on February 17, 1801, just a few weeks before the presidential inauguration. (The Twelfth Amendment, adopted in 1804 in response to this disastrous election, provided for separate balloting for president and vice president.)

Burr's seeming willingness to seize the presidency permanently soured his relationship with Jefferson, and made it unlikely that he would remain on the ticket in 1804. But Burr himself put the final nail in his political coffin in the summer of 1804 when he challenged Alexander Hamilton to a duel. The two men had been longtime political adversaries in New York, and Burr believed, not unreasonably, that Hamilton had uttered disparaging comments about him. When they met for the "affair of honor" at the dueling field in Weehawken, New Jersey, Burr's bullet fatally wounded Hamilton, and Burr quickly fled the scene, soon finding himself under indictment for murder in New Jersey and in his home state of New York.* Any hope of future national political office had now permanently vanished.

But Burr was a man of restless, relentless ambition, and he was not inclined to accept defeat. Stymied politically in the east, he came to believe that his best prospects now lay in the American West (which, in those days, meant the area between the Appalachian Mountains and the Mississippi River). Between 1805 and 1806, Burr traveled throughout the region, sizing up locations and meeting with prominent individuals. He was clearly up to something, but what?

Burr's precise intentions were a mystery to his fellow Americans, and historians have debated the issue endlessly. The most favorable interpretation to Burr suggests that he was assembling a group of men to attack Mexico in the event of a war with Spain. The least favorable interpretation is that Burr intended to use armed force to attack the American city of New Orleans, and then sever the western United States from the east, creating an independent country with himself as the emperor. And there are a host of possibilities in between.

For President Jefferson, the case was clear: Burr had committed treason. In June 1807, a grand jury in Richmond,

* The dueling field is just across the Hudson River from what is now New York City's Theater District, where the duel concludes each presentation of the musical *Hamilton*.

Virginia, issued an indictment charging that Burr had levied war against the United States at Blennerhassett Island with a group of armed men, and then descended down the Ohio River with the intent to take possession of the American city of New Orleans.[6] Yet all sides agreed that Aaron Burr had been hundreds of miles away from Blennerhassett Island when the events charged in the indictment occurred. So why did the federal government charge Burr with committing treason in this remote and unlikely location?

Left to its own devices, the Jefferson administration would have tried the case differently, but several prior judicial decisions had significantly limited its options. Two of Burr's associates, Erick Bollman and Samuel Swartwout, had been detained on suspicion of treason in the District of Columbia. They filed a petition for a writ of habeas corpus (the legal mechanism by which people who feel they have been unlawfully detained can present their arguments to a court), arguing that their alleged crimes did not amount to treason.

The issue ultimately reached the United States Supreme Court in the case known as *Ex parte Bollman*, one of only a handful of treason cases ever decided by the Supreme Court. The Court's opinion, authored by Chief Justice John Marshall, agreed with the Jefferson administration that a purpose to "overturn the government of the United States in New Orleans" was unquestionably treasonable.[7] But the Court followed English precedent to hold that a mere conspiracy to levy war is not treason; there must be an actual levying of war.[8] The Court noted, however, that if war is actually levied, all persons who played a role in the conspiracy and performed "any part, however minute," are "to be considered as traitors."[9]

This holding would have significant implications for the Burr prosecution. In April 1807, relying on the *Bollman* decision, Chief Justice Marshall had declined to commit Burr to jail on a treason charge. The government had produced evidence of a conspiracy at most, but no evidence of an actual levying of war. Marshall found that failure perplexing, stating, "The assembling of forces to levy war is a visible transaction and numbers must witness it. It is therefore capable of proof."[10]

Marshall's ruling meant the Jefferson administration had to allege an actual levying of war tied directly to Aaron Burr. And the only place where that could have conceivably happened was Blennerhassett Island. About thirty men had assembled on the island as part of Burr's scheme. Even though Burr wasn't physically present, he was the ringleader of the conspiracy and had arranged for the men to be there. Thus, under this new theory, the actions of these men could be legally attributed to Burr; even though he wasn't physically present on the island, he was "constructively present," and could be found guilty of treason if the men on Blennerhassett Island had levied war against the United States.

Burr's subsequent trial was one of the most momentous events of the early nineteenth century. It was held in the Virginia state capitol, a building designed by Thomas

Jefferson and modeled on a Roman temple in France. Jefferson took a strong personal interest in the prosecution, sending detailed letters to federal attorneys on nearly every aspect of the case.[11] The Jefferson administration spared no expense; total costs for Burr's treason trial exceeded $100,000, over $4 million in today's currency.[12] Chief Justice John Marshall presided, along with United States District Judge Cyrus Griffin. Until the late nineteenth century, Supreme Court justices were required to "ride circuit," meaning that they presided over trials in the circuits to which they were assigned. Marshall's circuit included his hometown of Richmond.

Jury selection began on August 4, 1807, and consumed nearly two weeks, due to the difficulty of finding jurors who had not formed an opinion of Burr's guilt. The prosecution presented fourteen witnesses, many of whom were ably cross-examined by Burr himself. The defense then moved to stop the trial on the ground that no legally sufficient evidence of treason had been presented.

The attorneys on both sides presented extensive arguments on this question, and on August 31, 1807, Chief Justice Marshall announced his decision, the longest judicial opinion he ever wrote.[13] Marshall held that it was not sufficient to show that Burr had arranged for the assemblage of men on the island; at most, that showed a conspiracy to levy war. Rather, the government had to prove an overt act on Burr's part showing actual levying of war. That act "may be minute, it may not be the actual appearance in arms, and it may be remote from the scene of action . . .

but it must be a part, and that part must be performed by the person who is leagued in the conspiracy."[14] Marshall therefore required the prosecution to come forward with evidence of actual acts of levying war that had occurred on Blennerhassett Island and that could be directly tied to Burr. The government had no such evidence, and the case was submitted directly to the jury without any presentation of witnesses for the defense.

The jury foreman (who, curiously, was John Marshall's brother-in-law) announced the verdict: "We the jury say that Aaron Burr is not proved to be guilty under this indictment by any evidence submitted to us. We therefore find him not guilty."[15] Burr objected to the form of this verdict, because the phrase "by any evidence submitted to us" was highly irregular, but Marshall directed that it be entered as a "not guilty" verdict. The jury's peculiar phrasing of the verdict indicated that it had some doubts as to Burr's actual innocence, but his guilt had not been proven to its satisfaction. In response to Marshall's ruling and the jury's verdict, the government dropped the remaining treason charges against six of Burr's associates.[16]

President Jefferson was predictably furious about Marshall's handling of the trial, complaining that Marshall's ruling had issued a "proclamation of impunity" to every treasonable combination.[17] In Baltimore, a mob hung Marshall in effigy for his "strange capers in open court."[18] But most historians have praised Marshall for his balanced handling of a difficult political trial. He was placed in a nearly impossible position, and his rulings were careful, thoughtful, and have stood the test of time. Even more significant, Marshall's conduct demonstrated the importance of an independent federal judiciary that was not cowed by the executive branch and that proved itself fully capable of protecting the rights of even the most unpopular defendants.

Although Burr had escaped conviction for treason, his life continued to spiral downhill. After spending several years in Europe, during which he tried to persuade foreign governments to support further schemes against Mexico, Burr returned to the United States. The death of his only grandson, followed shortly by the death of his only acknowledged child, a daughter, left him without any legitimate descendants (there seem to have been others that remained unacknowledged, including two children with a woman of color[19]). Burr resumed his legal practice in New York, where he worked quietly until his death in 1836.

One of the great mysteries of American history is what Burr really intended on his western travels. Most of the evidence suggests that he was up to no good. And he acted guilty—despite his impressive legal talents, he consistently refused to take actions or make statements that could have easily cleared away suspicion. Revelations from foreign archives have confirmed that Burr solicited both the Spanish and British governments in attempts to divide the United States.[20] On balance, he was clearly disloyal to his country.

The jurors who acquitted Burr did not have access to all of this evidence, but even if they had, it may not have proven an actual act of treason. The men at Blennerhassett Island might have later been employed to levy war against the United States, but they were doing nothing illegal on the island itself. At most, there was a conspiracy that had yet to ripen into full-fledged treason. That said, the men were well positioned to do significant damage, and it's possible they might have done so very quickly. Attorney David Stewart, in a careful review of the evidence, concludes that Burr intended to create an uprising in New Orleans with the eventual goal of installing himself as emperor of a new western nation.[21]

Another possibility is suggested by historian Peter Hoffer, who argues that Burr's various activities may have amounted to little more than a giant confidence game—a scheme to raise money for himself by telling every potential supporter what he wanted to hear. The inconsistency and mystery of Burr's motives were thus critical to ensnaring more and more financial backing.[22] Burr was not a traitor, but simply a con man working his marks in the American West.

The reality is that we will never know for sure precisely what Burr intended. His inner thoughts were shrouded in obscurity, even to his contemporaries. But the fall of Aaron Burr, although resembling a Hollywood thriller, also has echoes of a Greek tragedy. A man who was once a soaring political star—almost elected president of the United States at the age of forty-five—found himself just a few years later undone by his own ambition, indicted for murder, and tried for treason against his own country. It is a cautionary tale about vanity and hubris, but also a useful reminder that no one—not even a former vice president or a president who prosecutes him—is above the law.

5

The Forgotten Crime of Treason Against a State

One of the less-known features of American treason law is that the offense is not limited to treason against the United States. Forty-three states define the offense of treason against them, either in their state constitutions or in a criminal statute.[1] Oregon's statute is typical: "A person commits the crime of treason if the person levies war against the State of Oregon or adheres to its enemies, giving them aid and comfort."[2]

Prior to the adoption of our current Constitution, all treason prosecutions were undertaken at the state level. The Articles of Confederation, our first national constitution, did not provide for a federal court system, leaving state prosecutions to fill the void. For example, Pennsylvania prosecuted a number of people during the American

Revolution for treason against the state of Pennsylvania.[3] But despite state-level prosecution, the offense was generally perceived as national in scope. Throughout the Revolution, people regularly referred to the offense of "treason against the United States."[4] Benedict Arnold, for example, was widely reviled as a traitor, not primarily against his home state, but against the United States as a whole.

Since the adoption of the United States Constitution and the creation of federal treason law, state treason prosecutions have been a rarity. Attorney J. Taylor McConkie, who has written the most extensive modern analysis of state treason laws, notes, "State treason laws are like a rusty tool in the backyard shed: we have a vague sense that the tool was useful at some point, so we would rather not discard it; but for now, we cannot imagine why we need it or how it ought to be used."[5]

State treason laws are indeed a rusty tool today, but we must remember that the metal was once sharply polished and honed to a razor's edge. The cases of the men convicted under these laws are among the most fascinating in American legal history: Thomas Wilson Dorr, a lawyer who claimed to be the governor of Rhode Island, convicted of treason against that state in 1844; the antislavery fighters John Brown and Edwin Coppoc, executed for treason against Virginia in 1859 after the failed raid on Harpers Ferry; and Walter Allen, a union leader convicted of treason against West Virginia in the early 1920s. All these defendants were animated by broad visions of social reform—visions that have largely been vindicated in the court of history. At the time, however, their causes were viewed as deeply threatening to entrenched interests, and they were accordingly prosecuted, not just as ordinary criminals, but as traitors against their states.

What happens when there are two governments in a state, both claiming to be legitimate? This perplexing question confronted Rhode Island in the early 1840s.

Of the original thirteen states, eleven adopted new constitutions after the Declaration of Independence. Only Connecticut and Rhode Island did not, choosing instead to be governed by their colonial charters. Connecticut finally adopted a constitution in 1818, but by 1841 Rhode Island was still governed by its 1663 charter, adopted nearly 180 years previously. Significantly, the charter's allocation of representatives had not been updated to accommodate changes in population, and the charter government restricted suffrage to men who held a certain amount of real property.

The charter made significant political change impossible, and a popular movement arose in support of a constitutional convention to replace it. In the fall of 1841, the People's Convention, composed of elected delegates, drafted a new constitution for Rhode Island.[6] The resulting document, called the "People's Constitution," resolved the apportionment problems and guaranteed suffrage for all white adult males. The delegates arranged for a ratifying election to be held in December 1841. The expanded electorate approved the constitution by a vote of 13,947 to 52.[7]

The legislature of the charter government, however, denounced the People's Constitution as illegal and enacted a law defining the exercise of office under it as a "usurpation of the sovereign power of this State" and an act of "treason against the state," punishable by life imprisonment.[8]

The supporters of the People's Constitution argued that their new constitution was now the governing law of Rhode Island, and they organized elections for April 18, 1842, under its provisions. Elected to the governor's chair (which the People's Constitution made significantly more powerful than under the 1663 charter) was a short, pudgy lawyer named Thomas Wilson Dorr.

Dorr was an unlikely leader of a popular movement. Born into a wealthy aristocratic family in Providence, he had earned a mathematics degree at Harvard College before entering into a legal career.[9] His own parents discouraged him from seeking office under the People's Constitution, warning him that his candidacy would bring "shame and disgrace" to his family and "hurry us sorrowing to the grave."[10] But Dorr had helped draft the People's Constitution, and he was determined to make its reforms effective.

The new government was organized on May 3, 1842. Dorr was sworn in as governor and delivered an inaugural address. The legislature convened, divided its members into committees, and enacted various legislative measures, including a repeal of the law that made it treason to serve under the People's Constitution. But the new government did not attempt to occupy the state capitol, which would have given it a more visible stamp of legitimacy, and instead conducted its business at a nearby foundry.

Two weeks later, Dorr determined that military action was necessary for his government to achieve firm control of the state. The state arsenal was held by the charter government, and Dorr and his supporters launched an unsuccessful attack (at the critical moment, a cannon failed to ignite). Fearing arrest by charter forces, Dorr fled the state, and much of his political support evaporated. Although he returned to Rhode Island in June and briefly attempted to rally forces against the charter government, his movement was clearly at an end. Dorr again fled the state, and the "Dorr Rebellion," as it came to be known, was over.

Dorr nonetheless remained in serious legal jeopardy. On August 25, 1842, he was indicted by a Newport grand jury for treason against the state of Rhode Island. When he voluntarily returned to the state in October 1843, he was immediately arrested. In April 1844, Dorr's trial for treason began in Newport.

Dorr wasn't the first man tried for treason against Rhode Island. In the fall of 1842, the state had prosecuted Franklin Cooley, a Providence stonecutter who had served as a representative in the People's Legislature. Cooley was charged under the statute that made it treason to serve under the People's Constitution. The case ended in a hung jury, however, and the state did not retry him.[11]

Dorr, by contrast, was charged with treason by levying war against the state of Rhode Island based on the May 1842 attack on the arsenal and the June 1842 attempt to rally forces against the state. The prosecution condemned Dorr as a man who had "waged war on the sanctities of private life, for the accomplishment of his foul, ambitious, and nefarious purposes; to attain which he was ready and willing to imbue his hands in the blood of his friends and relatives. . . . [H]e had attempted with his own hands to light the torch of civil war against his relations and fellow-citizens."[12] Dorr's counsel responded that Dorr had been acting as the legally elected governor of the state and his conduct could not constitute treason. The court found this argument inadmissible and significantly restricted the defense's ability to present evidence to support it. The jury agreed upon their guilty verdict "immediately," since, as one juror explained, "There was nothing for us to do, the Court made everything plain for us."[13] The sentence was life imprisonment at hard labor.

By most measures, the Dorr Rebellion ended in failure—the People's Constitution was never implemented, and its leader was convicted of treason. But the momentum for political reform unleashed by the Rebellion led the charter government to finally approve the drafting of a new state constitution. In November 1842, Rhode Island voters ratified the document, ending Rhode Island's peculiar status as the last state still governed by a colonial charter. The new constitution granted some, but by no means all, of the reforms that had been included in the People's Constitution. In 1845, a new political coalition, dubbed the "Liberation Whigs" (so called because they supported liberating Dorr from prison), gained control of the state legislature and quickly enacted a law granting pardons to all the individuals convicted as a result of the Dorr Rebellion. Twenty months after his initial arrest, Thomas Wilson Dorr was again a free man.

For constitutional lawyers, the Dorr Rebellion is primarily remembered for its role in the 1849 U.S. Supreme Court decision in *Luther v. Borden*.[14] The Court was asked to determine whether the charter government or the People's Government was the legitimate government of Rhode Island in 1842. The Court refused to answer, concluding that it had no authority to resolve the question. The U.S. Constitution, the Court held, made Congress and the president—not the federal courts—the final arbiters of the legitimacy of state governments.

Like Thomas Wilson Dorr, John Brown was also a proponent of political reform, but he was willing to take even more radical actions in support of his vision. On the night of October 16, 1859, Brown and eighteen armed men crossed the Potomac River from Maryland and seized the federal arsenal in the small town of Harpers Ferry, Virginia (now part of West Virginia). Brown's intent was to trigger a widespread slave revolt, which would ultimately lead to the abolition of slavery. The scheme was poorly planned, clumsily executed, and doomed to failure. It was quickly suppressed by federal troops led by Robert E. Lee and J. E. B. Stuart, but not without significant bloodshed. The raiders killed five men and wounded nine more, and ten of the raiders perished in the assault.[15]

For the state of Virginia, the raid was a terrifying violation of the state's sovereignty. Although Brown had targeted only the federal arsenal, and thus seemingly waged war only against the institutions of the federal government, state prosecutors quickly indicted Brown and several of his associates for treason against the state of Virginia, as well as for murder and conspiracy. Virginia law defined treason to include levying war against the state, and the treason count duly included this charge. But Virginia law differed from federal law in that it also singled out establishing an independent government within the state as a distinct form of treason. Brown and his associates were charged with this form of treason as well, based on Brown's drafting of a "Provisional Constitution," under which he claimed to serve as commander in chief.[16] President James Buchanan was pleased to leave the entire matter in the hands of Virginia authorities, and ten days after the raid collapsed, Brown's trial began at the Jefferson County Courthouse in nearby Charlestown, Virginia.

The trial was a national media sensation, the first genuine "trial of the century." A telegraph line was specially constructed to Charlestown, enabling reports of the trial to be spread instantaneously throughout the country. For the first time, Americans could read blow-by-blow accounts of an ongoing criminal trial in their daily newspapers.[17]

The outcome, though, was never really in doubt. No Virginia jury was going to acquit John Brown—and especially not the jury empaneled in Brown's case. The nine slaveholders on the jury owned fifty-five enslaved people between them.[18] After five days of trial, the jury took only forty-five minutes to find Brown guilty on all counts, and on November 2, 1859, he was sentenced to death. Another raider, Edwin Coppoc, was also convicted on the same counts of treason, murder, and conspiracy, and both men were executed in December 1859.[19]

In the audience at Brown's hanging was a young actor named John Wilkes Booth. Booth was glad to see the "traitor" hanged, but he later admitted to a grudging admiration for Brown's boldness, claiming "John Brown was a man inspired, the grandest character of this century!"[20] The man Booth would later assassinate, Abraham Lincoln, agreed that Brown had been lawfully convicted: "Old John Brown has just been executed for treason against a state. We cannot object, even though he agreed with us in thinking slavery wrong. That cannot excuse violence, bloodshed, and treason."[21]

Of course, the murder charges were more than enough to send Brown and Coppoc to their doom. Why did Virginia prosecutors include a treason charge? It made a powerful political statement about the significance of the raid, but it also eliminated the possibility of a pardon from Virginia's governor, Henry Wise, who was viewed as overly emotional and unpredictable. Although Virginia governors could freely grant pardons in other capital cases, Virginia law required the assent of the General Assembly before a pardon could be issued for a treason conviction.[22]

Brown and Coppoc lost both their trials and their lives, but their cause, like Dorr's, was ultimately vindicated. Shortly before his death, Brown stated that he was "quite certain that the crimes of this guilty land will never be purged away, but with blood."[23] Four years of civil war would stain the land with blood, but six years after Brown's execution, the Thirteenth Amendment would finally fulfill

Brown's vision of eradicating slavery throughout the United States.

Over sixty years after Brown and Coppoc marched to the gallows, the same little courthouse in Charlestown, now part of West Virginia, was again teeming with people eager to watch another treason trial. In 1922, the state of West Virginia indicted twenty-four men for the offense of treason by levying war against the state. The cases arose from the so-called Mine Wars, a series of violent disputes between labor and management in West Virginia's coal country. In response to a miners' strike, the governor of West Virginia had declared martial law in Mingo County and had imprisoned over a hundred striking miners and union leaders. A large army of miners, eventually numbering over eight thousand, mustered in nearby Boone County, with the intent of marching through Logan County on their way to rescue the imprisoned men in Mingo County and end martial law. In response, the sheriff of Logan County summoned a counter-army of over three thousand men, equipped with a vast arsenal of weapons and even aircraft, which were used to bomb the miners' positions.

It was an extraordinary scene. As historian James Green has noted, the miners' army represented the "largest civil insurrection the country had experienced since the Civil War. . . . After five months in office, President Warren G. Harding was confronted with an almost unimaginable scenario: two armies of civilians—both filled with veterans of the Great War in Europe—were prepared to engage in mortal combat on American soil just two hundred miles from the nation's capital."[24] On August 31, 1921, the much-dreaded conflict finally erupted in what became known as the Battle of Blair Mountain. The fighting continued for three more days, in scattered other mountain locations, until federal troops finally quelled the dispute on September 4. Despite an enormous expenditure of ammunition, casualties were low on both sides. Although the precise number is not known, one modern estimate is that approximately sixteen people died in the fighting.[25]

The state government, heavily controlled by powerful coal interests, was outraged by the miners' actions and was determined to prosecute the leaders. In addition to the more obvious charges of murder and conspiracy, state authorities indicted twenty-four men for treason against the state of West Virginia by levying war against it.

Many observers were highly skeptical of the state's resort to treason charges. The county prosecutor initially assigned to the cases chose to resign rather than pursue charges that he deemed legally inappropriate and "mean-spirited" (he was replaced by attorneys hired by the coal companies). The *New York Times* complained that "in West Virginia indictments for treason seem to be thrown about as carelessly as if they were indictments for the larceny of a chicken."[26] Even the presiding judge appeared to have some doubts, although he ultimately upheld the legality of the charges.

Although the normal venue for the cases would have been in either Boone or Logan County, defense lawyers successfully persuaded the prosecutors and judges to have the trials moved to Charlestown, the county seat of Jefferson County. William Blizzard, described as the "generalissimo" of the miner's army, was the first man put on trial. After over three weeks of testimony and arguments, Blizzard was acquitted.

Prosecutors were more successful with the second trial, that of Walter Allen, president of a union local, who was convicted and sentenced to ten years in prison. Members of Allen's jury had admitted to anti-union bias, and his case appears to have had fewer factual complications than Blizzard's. Allen bears the significant distinction of being the only person convicted for treason against a state in the twentieth century, as well as the only twentieth-century American convicted on a levying-war charge, as opposed to an aiding-the-enemy charge. The United Mine Workers posted bail for Allen, pending his appeal, which would have raised significant questions about the scope of West Virginia's treason law. But Allen skipped bail and was never heard from again, leaving the legal issues unresolved.[27]

The third person in line for trial was Frank Keeney, another prominent union leader. But the presiding judge concluded that the political climate in Jefferson County had so turned against the miners that it was impossible to seat an unbiased jury. After the judge ordered the trial moved to Morgan County, the prosecution abandoned the case against Keeney, fearing that the new venue made a conviction impossible. All the treason charges against the other defendants were then quietly dismissed, although several unsuccessful prosecutions for other offenses continued.[28] With that, the most recent treason charges to be brought by a state government came to an end.

Although the miners had lost the battle, they ultimately won the war. President Franklin Roosevelt's New Deal finally brought unionization to the West Virginia coal country after decades of failure. No longer would miners need to form an army to assert their rights against the state.[29]

Underlying all the state treason prosecutions was a fundamental question: Did states have any authority to punish the offense of treason at all? After all, one could argue that the United States Constitution reserves treason prosecutions solely to the federal government. The notion of treason against Oregon, for example, seems, on the surface, as implausible as Oregon holding a seat in the United Nations.

The power of states to prosecute treason was a question that vexed even the delegates to the Constitutional Convention. Connecticut delegate William Johnson took the most extreme position, arguing that states had no power over treason, even under the Articles of Confederation, because sovereignty rested in the Union alone. By contrast, Virginia delegate George Mason pointed out that "an act may be treason against a particular state which is not so against the United States," such as Bacon's Rebellion in Virginia.[30]

The defendants who faced state treason charges after the adoption of the Constitution all insisted that only the federal government could prosecute cases of treason—indeed, this was often their primary argument, one that would allow them to escape conviction even if they had committed all the underlying acts with which they had been charged. But the courts were unpersuaded, relying on three broad arguments to support the state prosecutions.

The first, and most straightforward, argument rested on a plain reading of the Constitution's text. Article III defines "Treason against the United States," but does not specifically limit the offense of treason against states; presumably if the document had intended to restrict state authority over treason it would have said so. Moreover, the Extradition Clause of Article IV refers to persons "charged in any State with Treason, Felony, or other Crime," a phrasing that would make little sense if states had no authority to initiate treason charges.[31]

The second argument was historical, pointing to the debates in the Constitutional Convention, which appeared to leave this matter to the states. A proposal to give Congress the "sole" power to punish treason, for example, was defeated, six states to five. Moreover, courts noted that most states criminalize treason against the state. The states that consistently enacted these laws must have assumed that they were constitutionally authorized to do so.

The final argument was more pragmatic, pointing out that states have the ability to defend themselves against internal insurrections. The judge in the West Virginia mine case, for example, argued that "it would be a strange condition indeed if that Government should be vested with all the authority and power necessary to protect every individual within its borders, and yet be denied the power to protect its own life."[32]

All these decisions assumed that the underlying conduct was an act of levying war solely against the state government, without any corresponding attack on federal institutions (which would have triggered federal law). In the midst of the Dorr Rebellion, United States Supreme Court Justice Joseph Story explained that treason "may be, and often is, aimed altogether against the sovereignty of a particular state." For example, if people assemble to "overturn the government or constitution of a state," but with no interference with the federal government, it is "treason against the state, and against the state only."[33] Since federal treason law does not apply to this conduct, states must be free to conduct their own prosecutions.

But what if the charge is not levying war against the state, as was the case in the Dorr Rebellion, John Brown's Raid, and the Mine Wars, but adhering to the state's enemies, giving them aid and comfort? Many states include this offense in their treason statutes, but prosecutions have been vanishingly rare and they are almost certainly unconstitutional.

The leading case arose during the War of 1812, when the state of New York indicted several men for treason against the state of New York for aiding the forces of Great Britain. In *People v. Lynch*, a New York state court dismissed the indictment, concluding that "Great Britain cannot be said to be at war with the state of New York, in its aggregate and political capacity."[34] Great Britain was at war with the United States, not with New York, and it was for the United States alone to punish this form of treason. A similar conclusion had been reached just a few years after the adoption of the Constitution by Massachusetts chief justice Francis Dana, who concluded that the Constitution had eliminated the state's ability to punish treason by aiding the enemy.[35]

The decision in *Lynch* seems intuitively correct. Under our federal constitution, states have no role to play in foreign affairs, which are entirely entrusted to the federal government. States cannot declare war, engage in attacks on foreign countries, or negotiate treaties of peace. Thus, states themselves cannot have "enemies" in any meaningful sense of the word. Any enemy of a state would also be an enemy of the United States, and aid to such an enemy would be subject to federal treason law.

But so long as they are dealing with internal issues, states have considerable latitude to define the scope of treason against the state.[36] The federal government is bound by Article III's extremely narrow definition of treason. But the states are not. If a state wanted to, it could define bribery and corruption by state officials as treason against the state. It could define election fraud as treason. It could even define burglary of the state capitol as treason. There are strong prudential reasons against doing this, of course, and the Eighth Amendment would prevent states from imposing the death penalty for these offenses.[37] But if a state was determined to use the term "treason" in a more expansive manner, nothing in the United States Constitution stands in the way.

So—treason against Oregon for stuffing a ballot box? It's possible. But I wouldn't hold my breath waiting for it to happen.

6

The Case of Castner Hanway and the Fugitive Slave Act

No building in America is more central to the story of treason than Independence Hall in Philadelphia. The tourists who visit during peak months are allowed to view the Assembly Room, where the Constitutional Convention drafted the Treason Clause. Across the center passageway, they can also enter the Pennsylvania Supreme Court room, where several trials for treason were conducted during the Revolutionary War.[1]

Few tourists make it up to the second floor of the building, which is only open during less crowded times. But it is well worth seeing. Here, one can find the Long Gallery, an elegant corridor that hosted dinners and receptions in the eighteenth century. One can also view the

Committee of the Assembly Chamber and the Governor's Council Chamber, both restored to eighteenth-century splendor. Nothing in the display indicates that anything significant happened here in the nineteenth century.

On November 24, 1851, however, Philadelphians were desperate to get into the Governor's Council Chamber. Shortly after nine a.m., an "immense crowd of blacks and whites" filled the lower floor of Independence Hall, all seeking a seat in the chamber, which was now serving as a United States federal court.[2] The day's court calendar promised to be riveting. Thirty-eight men had been indicted for treason against the United States—the most ever indicted for treason at the same time since the Constitution was adopted. Even the Whiskey Rebellion of 1794, which saw thousands of men in arms against the government, yielded only twenty-four indictments.[3] On numbers alone, these trials had the potential to be the most significant treason cases in American history.

But there was something else that made the cases profoundly important. Thirty-four of the thirty-eight defendants were African-Americans. To this day, they remain the only African-Americans ever indicted for treason against the United States under the Constitution. And the trials had generated enormous public attention because they concerned one of the most explosive issues in American politics—the Fugitive Slave Act of 1850.[4]

The fame attached to the so-called Underground Railroad in modern times has occasionally led to misapprehensions about the legal status of escaping slaves. Many Americans, I suspect, still believe that an enslaved person became free by escaping from a slave state into a free state. But this was emphatically not the case. Indeed, the very possibility was specifically rejected in the Constitution itself. Article IV, Section Two stated:

> *No Person held to Service or Labour in one State, under the Laws thereof, escaping into another, shall, in Consequence of any Law or Regulation therein, be discharged from such Service or Labour, but shall be delivered up on Claim of the Party to whom such Service or Labour may be due.*

Under this provision, known as the "Fugitive Slave Clause," escaping to a free state did not change the enslaved person's legal status. To be truly free from the American laws of slavery, an enslaved person needed to reach Canada.

The Fugitive Slave Clause generated significant controversy, including disputes over whether it was self-executing and whether it imposed any duties on states to assist in returning escaped slaves. In 1793, Congress passed a Fugitive Slave Act to enforce the clause, but by the 1840s it had become relatively easy to evade. So as part of the celebrated Compromise of 1850, which, among other things, admitted California to the Union as a free state, Congress enacted a stronger Fugitive Slave Act. Under the new Act, commissioners were appointed by federal courts to hear cases involving alleged escaped slaves. There were no jury trials, the accused persons could not testify, and the proceedings often amounted to little more than rubber-stamping the affidavit of someone claiming to be a slave owner. Commissioners received a $10 fee if they ruled in favor of the claimant, but only a $5 fee if they ruled in favor of the alleged slave. The Act put free blacks in the North in serious jeopardy, as it was easy for them to be falsely accused of being escaped slaves. In courtrooms across the country, white men from the South wielded affidavits claiming to be the owners of African-Americans in the North. In Philadelphia, the Act was enforced from 1850 to 1854 on the second floor of Independence Hall, where the United States federal court was sitting. The irony of this location was not lost on contemporary observers. An African-American newspaper complained bitterly about enforcement of the Fugitive Slave Act in the very building where the words "all men are created equal" had been adopted.[5]

The path to the 1851 treason trials in Independence Hall began just across the Mason-Dixon Line, at the Maryland farm of a slave owner named Edward Gorsuch. (The farm was a short walk from Milton Academy, where a young John Wilkes Booth was attending school with one of Gorsuch's sons.[6]) Edward had been the most historically significant member of the Gorsuch family until 2017, when Neil Gorsuch, his third cousin, five times removed, was appointed to the United States Supreme Court.[7]

In November 1849, Edward discovered that four of the enslaved men working on his farm—Noah Buley, Nelson Ford, Joshua Hammond, and George Hammond—had disappeared. The men were between nineteen and twenty-two years of age, and Gorsuch had arranged for them to be freed when they turned twenty-eight, an act that he expected would earn him their unconditional loyalty. For nearly two years, Gorsuch had no information on their whereabouts, but in late August 1851 he received a letter suggesting that the men were living near the town of Christiana, in Lancaster County, Pennsylvania. Armed with the provisions of the new Fugitive Slave Act, Gorsuch and five other men traveled to Pennsylvania and secured warrants for the escaped slaves from a commissioner. They also secured the assistance of two Philadelphia policemen and Deputy United States Marshal Henry H. Kline, who agreed to help with any potential arrests.

Kline, however, provided more hindrance than help. He did little to disguise his movements toward Christiana, and word of his pending arrival quickly reached the town's large free African-American community, eliminating the possibility of the escaped men being taken by surprise. When the Philadelphia policemen learned that their movements had been discovered, they abandoned the operation and returned home.

In the early morning of September 11, 1851, a local informant led the Gorsuch party to the two-story stone house of William Parker, a former slave and leader of the local African-American self-protection society. They had been told that two of Gorsuch's slaves were hiding in the house. As historian Thomas Slaughter notes, "Whatever his goals, the guide delivered his employers as if on a platter to the very seat of Lancaster's antislavery resistance. Nowhere in the county would the posse have been more in danger for their very lives than on the doorstep of the stone house that was William Parker's home."[8]

Accounts vary as to what precisely happened in the ensuing maelstrom, but the broad outlines are reasonably clear. Gorsuch and Kline initially attempted to execute the warrants and entered the house, but they quickly retreated after the occupants hurled a large object at them. Parker's wife ascended to the attic, where she blew a horn, the customary method for the members of the self-protection society to summon assistance from one another. At this point, the occupants of the house and the Gorsuch party began exchanging gunshots, but the firing stopped when the occupants asked for time to think things over, a ruse designed to buy time until others could arrive.

The horn did its work. Large numbers of armed African-Americans began arriving at the Parker house, along with several white men, including a miller named Castner Hanway, Parker's closest neighbor, who arrived on horseback, but without any weapons. Marshal Kline sought Hanway's assistance, but Hanway refused to have anything do with the warrants and advised Kline to retreat. Kline, along with two others of the Maryland party, heeded this advice and fled the scene. Gorsuch then sought to approach the Parker house again, when he was confronted by one of the escaped slaves, who clubbed him on the head before shooting him to death. Other African-Americans then opened fire; Gorsuch's son Dickinson was shot at close range with a shotgun, and another member of the party incurred at least four bullet wounds. Castner Hanway initially tried to shield several of the Maryland men from violence, but fled the scene when one of the African-Americans told him he risked being killed himself.

Gorsuch's attempt to enforce the Fugitive Slave Act could not have ended more poorly. Not only was Gorsuch himself killed, his son was seriously wounded, and the escaped slaves and William Parker had fled. Parker and two of the slaves raced to Rochester, New York, and from there across Lake Ontario to Canada. Before leaving Rochester, Parker presented Gorsuch's gun to the famous abolitionist Frederick Douglass.

Not surprisingly, news of what became known as the "Christiana Riot" spread quickly across the country. Southerners were outraged and demanded that Gorsuch's killers be brought to justice. A Georgia newspaper complained, "Respectable citizens of the South are shot down like wild beasts, and a wagon and horses could not be procured to pursue the murderers."[9] A mass meeting in Baltimore, presided over by the city's mayor, unanimously resolved that the crime was not merely a "murder of the most barbarous character," but a "political offense affecting the whole nation, and a flagrant outrage upon the feelings and constitutional rights of every Southern man."[10] Lurid (and almost certainly false) accounts circulated that black women had brutally mutilated Gorsuch's body.

Crimes had clearly been committed, not the least of which was murder. But the men who had pulled the triggers had fled, and the remaining rioters were subject to lesser charges in Pennsylvania state court. Southerners nonetheless demanded that the rioters be charged with treason in federal court. This demand placed the administration of President Millard Fillmore in an awkward position. If the federal government obtained convictions for treason and executed the leading rioters, it would inflame Northern sensibilities and risk creating abolitionist martyrs. If it did nothing, however, the South would be convinced that the Fugitive Slave Act had effectively become a dead letter. The solution was to proceed with treason prosecutions, but to leave them almost entirely in the hands of United States Attorney John W. Ashmead, with minimal direction from anyone higher up in the administration. To assuage Maryland, the state's attorney general was allowed to appear as part of the prosecution team.[11]

Treason was not an obvious fit for the events at Christiana, but it was the only federal crime that was even remotely applicable. A very broad reading of precedents from the Whiskey Rebellion and Fries's Rebellion cases could perhaps support indictments for levying war against the United States, on the theory that the rioters had sought to suppress entirely the operation of a federal law by the use of force. It was not a strong argument, but it was all Ashmead had, and he was determined to go forward. He eventually procured indictments against thirty-four African-American men and four white men, including Castner Hanway.

As in the Aaron Burr case, the trial was held before two federal judges, in this case United States Supreme Court Justice Robert Grier and federal district judge John J. Kane. The defense had plenty of reason to be worried about Grier. A Pennsylvanian who had been elevated to the Supreme Court from almost complete obscurity by President James K. Polk, Grier was known for his strong pro-Southern views, including his strident support for the 1850 Fugitive Slave Act. Six years later, Grier would join Chief Justice Roger Taney's infamous opinion in the *Dred Scott* case, which held that African-Americans were barred from United States citizenship and that Congress lacked power to prohibit slavery in the territories.[12] Judge Kane, too, was worrisome for the defense, as he had delivered a grand jury charge that seemed to equate the Christiana Riot with treason.

The trials opened on Monday, November 24, 1851, and the first defendant to be tried was Castner Hanway. He was an odd choice for the first trial—he hadn't fired a weapon and had even tried to protect some of the Gorsuch party from violence. But the prosecutors seemed to believe that the resistance of the African-American community of Christiana to the Fugitive Slave Act must have been inspired by white agitators acting behind the scenes, and Hanway, the first white person to arrive on the scene and one of the few who arrived on a horse, seemed a likely suspect.

Jury selection consumed three days. The notoriety of the Christiana Riot made it particularly important to find jurors who had not formed conclusive opinions on the defendants' guilt and who did not hold idiosyncratic views on the meaning of treason. As Justice Grier noted, "The whole country has been agitated by questions as to what in application legal is 'treason.'"[13] In the end, twelve men, ranging in age from thirty-six to seventy-three, and representing seven different counties, were seated in the jury box.[14] Southerners would later argue that the entire process of jury selection had been tainted, because the United States marshal who summoned the jury, Anthony E. Roberts, owed his job to the political patronage of Thaddeus Stevens. Not only was Stevens a prominent antislavery congressman, he was now serving as Castner Hanway's lead defense counsel. Southerners would also point to another seeming irregularity. Two of the prosecution's key witnesses were African-American men who were being held by Marshal Roberts in protective custody. Two weeks before the trial, the men mysteriously escaped and were never heard from again.[15]

Once the trial got underway, the prosecution witnesses set forth the basic facts of the Christiana Riot.[16] For its part, the defense sought to undermine the credibility of the prosecution witnesses, particularly Marshal Kline. It introduced evidence showing that Hanway had moved to Christiana only three years earlier and never attended any antislavery meetings. Despite strong prosecution objections, the defense was also allowed to introduce evidence that Southern kidnappers had previously abducted free blacks from the neighborhood and dragged them into slavery in the South. If the rioters had thought they were resisting unlawful kidnappers, they would not have had the required intent to obstruct a federal statute.

The ultimate issue was not one of fact, but of law. Even assuming all of the prosecution's facts, did the alleged conduct amount to treason by levying war against the United States? When the incident was first reported in American newspapers, it was regularly described as a riot or as a murder, but not as treason. The great abolitionist Frederick Douglass, not surprisingly, felt that the "attempt to magnify this into a treason trial is somewhat ridiculous."[17] More surprisingly, even some Southerners agreed. A Georgia newspaper argued that the treason trials were "humbug and nonsense. The crime at Christiana was not treason—it was murder—and for that, and that alone, these wretches should now be tried. The charge of Treason cannot, and will not be proven."[18] A Baltimore newspaper concluded that "We have seen nothing yet to convince us that the outrage in question can be, by any ingenuity, tortured into an act of treason; and certainly not before a Pennsylvania jury."[19]

After the presentation of the evidence, this dispute over the meaning of treason would now be directly addressed. For the prosecution, John Ashmead argued that forcible resistance to the Fugitive Slave Act, with the intent of rendering it inoperative, amounted to levying of war against the United States. Ashmead's greatest difficulty lay in connecting Castner Hanway to the riot; he had no direct evidence of any preexisting connection between Hanway and the rioters. But Ashmead argued that the circumstantial evidence was sufficient: "If you see the stream which comes from the distant mountains, swollen and leaping along as if a deluge were pouring its waters through its channel, do you not know that the snows have melted at the source, and the rains have descended from the heavens?" So, too, in this case. "Can you not infer that he went there by pre-arrangement, and that he was known by the coloured people as a man who would stand by them, in their resistance of the laws?"[20]

The defense countered that if Hanway arrived at Parker's house with a lawful intent, "it is no treason, even though he did afterwards see with composure the laws violated, or even commit a murder." Moreover, treason required a "dignity in mischievous design that aims at the life of the government, or at least at the prostration of some branch of its power, by an armed opposition," none of which was present here.[21]

On December 11, 1851, the judges issued their final charge to the jury. Justice Grier began with statements broadly sympathetic to the prosecution. Grier noted that "the testimony in this case has clearly established that a most horrible outrage upon the laws of the country has been committed. A citizen of a neighboring state, while in the exercise of his undoubted rights guaranteed to him by the constitution and laws of the United States, has been foully murdered by an armed mob of negroes." Moreover, Grier blamed the riot on abolitionists from out of state, "infuriated fanatics and unprincipled demagogues" who "counsel a bloody resistance to the laws of the land." He pointedly praised the Fugitive Slave Act and warned that its undermining in the North could lead the South to "seek secession."[22]

But when Grier turned to the nature of treason, his charge took on a very different tone. Although acknowledging that some English precedents interpreted levying war more broadly, he argued that "the better opinion there at present seems to be that the term 'levying war' should be confined to insurrections and rebellions for the purposes of overturning the government by force and arms." Grier then dropped the hammer on the prosecution: it was the view of both judges that Hanway's alleged offenses did not amount to treason. There was no evidence of any previous agreement to undermine the Fugitive Slave Act, and there was no evidence showing that the intent of the riot was to undermine the act generally, rather than to protect particular men from possible kidnappers. It would be a "dangerous precedent," Grier warned, to extend the crime of treason to a case like this.[23]

Grier's ruling virtually guaranteed an acquittal, and the jury returned after less than fifteen minutes of deliberation. But it's possible the jury would have acquitted in any event. According to one account, the jurors stated in the courtroom "that their minds were all made up as soon as the testimony for the prosecution was closed."[24]

With the Hanway case in ruins, the federal government conceded defeat and dropped the treason charges against the remaining defendants. State authorities still hoped to proceed with trials in Lancaster County, but the men who had fired the weapons had all fled and there was no credible eyewitness testimony directly tying the remaining defendants to any of the crimes. The state, too, was forced to concede defeat, and no state charges were filed against any Christiana rioters.

The trial left a bitter aftertaste in the mouths of many. The attorney general of Maryland was disgusted with the proceedings in Philadelphia and filed a report denouncing the judges, the jury, and the marshal. In a similar vein, a Baltimore newspaper complained, "It would seem, from the result of this trial, that negroes may commit murder with impunity in particular sections of Pennsylvania, provided the murdered individual be a slaveholder, or be in pursuit of a fugitive slave."[25]

The precise nature of the Southern complaints bears emphasis. It was not rooted in objections to the federal government or to some mystical attachment to states' rights. If anything, Southerners wanted stricter federal enforcement of the federal Fugitive Slave Act, most especially in those Northern states that opposed it. The Northern states, Southerners insisted, were improperly relying on "states' rights" to thwart the implementation of federal law. Northern states, by contrast, contended that the Fugitive Slave Act should not supplant their own laws that provided greater procedural protections to accused slaves. (If this debate sounds vaguely familiar, it should—it has strong parallels to modern debates over the duties of state and local governments with respect to enforcement of federal immigration law.)

For many Northerners, the Castner Hanway trial was profoundly disturbing. A man who may have been entirely innocent of any crime, who wandered into an ongoing incident, had been tried by the federal government for the highest offense known to the law. The prosecutors appeared driven by political vengeance, hoping to score points on the contested issue of slavery. Even more troubling, the sensational trial on the second floor of Independence Hall had raised serious questions about the durability of the Union that had been so painstakingly crafted on the first floor. The storied building, like the nation to which it had given birth, now risked becoming a house divided against itself.

7

Who Is Subject to American Treason Law?

Can a citizen of France commit treason against the United States? Can a citizen of the United States commit treason against the United Kingdom? Most people, including most lawyers and judges, would instinctively answer, "No." A federal judge in New York, for example, recently stated that the Treason Clause "by definition can apply only to United States citizens."[1] Similarly, a prominent American law professor once wrote that treason can "be committed *only* by a citizen."[2]

But the judge and the law professor are wrong. Treason is technically not a breach of citizenship—it is a breach of allegiance. To be subject to American treason law, a person must first owe allegiance to the United States. But in some circumstances this duty of allegiance extends to noncitizens.

The law recognizes two kinds of allegiance: permanent and temporary. Permanent allegiance is the most familiar. All citizens owe permanent allegiance to the United States, and this duty carries with them wherever they go in the world. In World War II, for example, American citizens were charged with treason against the United States for acts that they committed in Japan, Germany, and Italy.

Temporary allegiance is different. Noncitizens present in the United States owe temporary allegiance to the United States so long as they remain within the country. And if noncitizens violate that allegiance by levying war against the United States or adhering to our enemies, they can be prosecuted for treason just as citizens are. Unlike permanent allegiance, however, temporary allegiance (or local allegiance, as it is sometimes called), dissolves once the noncitizen leaves the country.

This doctrine is centuries old. In the early seventeenth century, the famous English jurist Sir Edward Coke wrote that foreign subjects were "within the protection of the King" while they were in England; such persons owed a "local obedience to the King . . . and if they commit High Treason against the King, they shall be punished as Traitors."[3]

The United States Supreme Court's most extensive discussion of allegiance came in the 1873 case of *Carlisle v. United States*.[4] The Court stated that a citizen owed an "absolute and permanent allegiance to his government" up to the point at which he or she renounced citizenship and became a citizen of another country. By contrast, the noncitizen, "whilst domiciled in the country, owes a local and temporary allegiance, which continues during the period of his residence." The Court noted that this "obligation of temporary allegiance by an alien resident in a friendly country" was widely recognized as a general principle by most other nations.[5]

The pre-1873 cases tended to vacillate on the question of whether mere presence in the country is enough, or whether the noncitizen must be resident or domiciled in the country. But the Supreme Court in *Carlisle* approvingly cited a treatise on international law that stated, the rights of sovereignty "extend to all strangers [resident] therein, not only to those who are naturalized and to those who are domiciled therein, having taken up their abode with the intention of permanent residence, but also to those whose residence is transitory. All strangers are under the protection of the sovereign while they are within his territories, and owe a temporary allegiance in return for that protection."[6] The American rule thus suggests that the duty of temporary allegiance extends even to tourists and casual visitors.

A significant consequence of this doctrine is that the 9/11 terrorists may have committed treason, in addition to murder and other crimes. All of the terrorists were Saudi or Egyptian citizens, but they had lived in the United States for some time prior to the attacks. The attack on the Pentagon, at least, was a clear act of levying war against the United States. Since the terrorists were subject to a duty of temporary allegiance while living here, they can properly be described as traitors to the United States. Of course, they all died in the attacks, so none were ever tried. But any who survived might plausibly have been charged with treason.

There are several significant exceptions to the general rule that noncitizens owe temporary allegiance while present in the United States. The first concerns enemy soldiers. If a foreign army invades the United States, the foreign soldiers do not owe any allegiance to the United States, even though they are present within it. Why not? Because they do not receive any protection from the United States, and protection is required before any duty of allegiance attaches. The best historical example is the British soldiers who invaded the United States during the War of 1812 and set fire to Washington, DC. They were clearly levying war against the United States, but they weren't traitors to the United States—they had no allegiance to the United States and were receiving no protection from it.

The second exception concerns ambassadors. Although English jurists debated the question whether foreign ambassadors were subject to English treason law, the better view seems to be that they are not. As Sir Matthew Hale, a prominent English judge, explained, a foreign ambassador must always be dealt with "as an enemy by the law of war or nations, and not as a traitor."[7] Ambassadors are always under the protection of their home governments, and can't really be said to be under the protection of the government of the United States.

Historically, there was also a likely exception for members of American Indian tribes. Although the United States was frequently at war with these tribes, the federal government never prosecuted an American Indian for the crime of treason against the United States. Indeed, it was assumed that tribal members were not birthright citizens of the United States under the Fourteenth Amendment, because they weren't technically "under the jurisdiction" of the United States. In 1924, Congress granted American citizenship to members of the Indian tribes, and they then became fully subject to American treason law.

Dual citizenship presents special problems, but the general rule is that American law will hold a dual citizen to the same standard as a non–dual citizen. In 1952, the United States Supreme Court decided the case of Tomoya Kawakita, who was a dual citizen of Japan and the United States. Kawakita was living in Japan when the war with the United States broke out, and he was later employed as an interpreter at a prisoner-of-war camp. After the war, the United States charged him with treason for acts of cruelty against American prisoners.[8]

Kawakita argued that a person with dual nationality "can be guilty of treason only to the country where he resides, not to the other country which claims him as a national." The Supreme Court rejected that argument, concluding that American citizenship carries "obligations of allegiance as well as privileges and benefits." For dual citizens, those obligations "may at times be difficult to discharge," but one cannot adopt "fair-weather citizenship, retaining it for possible contingent benefits but meanwhile playing the part of the traitor." Accordingly, any acts hostile to the United States that Kawakita voluntarily performed constituted treason.[9]

Perhaps the most striking instance of American treason law being applied to noncitizens arose from the American occupation of the Philippines. Following the outbreak of the Spanish-American War in 1898, American forces conquered the Spanish colony of the Philippines. The peace treaty ending the war formally transferred the Philippines to the United States. A subsequent revolt by Filipino natives was brutally crushed by the United States military.[10]

The United States was no stranger to acquiring territory, as its significant expansion in the nineteenth century demonstrated. But prior expansions had all been accompanied by an extension of American citizenship to the territory's inhabitants. Racist perceptions of the residents of the former Spanish colonies, however, led the United States to deny them citizenship, as well as certain constitutional rights. In a series of cases called *The Insular Cases*, the United States Supreme Court blessed this discrimination, concluding that American citizenship was inconsistent with colonization. In a 1901 opinion, Justice Edward Douglass White stated, "it is doubtful if Congress would ever assent to the annexation of territory upon the condition that its inhabitants, however foreign they may be to our habits, traditions, and modes of life, shall become at once citizens of the United States."[11] These decisions placed the Filipinos—and the inhabitants of the other new territories—in a nebulous legal category. They were subject to the authority of the United States, but were not citizens of the United States, a status for which we now use the term "U.S. national."

A "Philippine Commission," appointed by President William McKinley and headed by future president William Howard Taft, soon enacted a treason statute for the territory. The statute defined treason as levying war against the United States or against the government of the Philippine Islands, or as adhering to their enemies, giving them aid and comfort. American officials used this authority to prosecute at least three Filipinos for treason.[12] As one justice of the Philippine Supreme Court explained, "the defendant was a resident in the Philippine Islands, and owed allegiance to the United States Government in the Philippine Islands."[13]

American officials had consistently refused to extend the right to jury trial to the Philippines, and the United States Supreme Court upheld this refusal in 1904. The Court reasoned that jury trials were unnecessary for the "civilized" part of the islands, since they were accustomed to Spanish jurisprudence, under which juries were unknown. The "uncivilized parts of the archipelago," the Court continued, "were wholly unfitted to recognize the right of trial by jury."[14] The treason trials had accordingly proceeded without juries, the only such trials under the authority of the federal government for which a jury trial was denied. Congress, however, did extend the two-witness requirement to treason trials in the Philippines, and at least two defendants had their convictions reversed for failure to comply with that requirement.[15]

Although the Spanish-American War and its aftermath is now largely forgotten, the United States continues to hold overseas territories—Puerto Rico, the U.S. Virgin Islands, Guam, the Commonwealth of the Northern Mariana Islands, and American Samoa. With one exception, the residents of these islands are all U.S. citizens and are subject to permanent allegiance to the United States. The exception is American Samoa, where, for complicated reasons, the inhabitants have rejected U.S. citizenship and retain the status of U.S. nationals.[16] Federal statutory law, however, holds that U.S. nationals owe permanent allegiance to the United States in the same manner as citizens.[17] The American Samoans are thus in the same distinctive legal position as the Filipinos were over a hundred years ago—not citizens of the United States, but nonetheless fully bound by American treason law.

Because the doctrine of temporary allegiance is so widely applied, American citizens can be subject to the treason laws of other countries when residing or traveling abroad. In 1797, an American citizen named David McLane was executed for high treason against the British government in Quebec.[18] And in 1885, an American citizen named Louis Riel was executed in Regina for treason against the Dominion of Canada.[19]

The most well-known case is that of William Joyce, colloquially known as "Lord Haw Haw," executed for treason against the United Kingdom for serving as a German radio propagandist during World War II.[20] Joyce had been born in the United States, and was thus a United States citizen by birth. Although he spent most of his life in the United Kingdom, he never became a naturalized British subject.

Joyce's attorneys argued that he could not be guilty of treason against the United Kingdom for his actions in Germany, because he did not owe permanent allegiance to the U.K. Once Joyce departed for Germany, they claimed, his temporary allegiance to the U.K. ended, and he was free to aid the Germans.

The British courts rejected this argument. Although they accepted the broad contours of the distinction between permanent and temporary allegiance, they ruled that in certain cases a nonsubject's duty of allegiance survived his departure from the country. Joyce's was such a case, because of one key distinction—although not a British subject, Joyce was using a British passport. As the Lord Chancellor put it, "the Crown in issuing a passport is assuming an onerous burden, and the holder of a passport is acquiring substantial privileges."[21] Joyce could not claim the benefits of the Crown's protection while rejecting any corresponding duty of allegiance. But the court concluded that the duty of allegiance expired with his passport (it had expired while he was in Germany); accordingly, the treason charges were based solely on Joyce's conduct in Germany while the passport was valid.[22]

Joyce's subsequent hanging on January 3, 1946, was doubly distinctive. He was the first (and only) United States citizen ever executed in the United Kingdom for the crime of treason.[23] But he was also the last person hanged in the U.K. for treason before the abolition of the death penalty. In other words, the last executed British traitor was actually an American—a vivid demonstration of the doctrine of temporary allegiance.

In the United States, the existence of state treason laws places a distinctive twist on the issue of allegiance. Do these laws require allegiance to the state, and, if so, how is that allegiance determined? Can a person who is not a citizen of a state be prosecuted for treason for an attack on that state? The issue has arisen only once, but the circumstances could not have been more dramatic—the trial of John Brown and his associates after the failed raid on Harpers Ferry, Virginia.[24]

Brown and his men had prepared for the raid in the neighboring state of Maryland, and when they launched their attack over the Potomac River, they arrived as soldiers, in open military hostility to the state of Virginia. There was thus a plausible argument that the men owed no allegiance to Virginia—they were analogous to members of an invading foreign army. Just as members of the British army owed no allegiance to the United States despite being present in the United States during the War of 1812, Brown's men owed no allegiance to Virginia despite being present within it.

Brown's attorneys made this argument, both at trial and on appeal, but the Virginia courts were unpersuaded.

The trial court's reasoning is not entirely clear, but it seemed to rely in part on the Privileges and Immunities Clause of Article IV of the U.S. Constitution, which states, "The Citizens of each State shall be entitled to all Privileges and Immunities of Citizens in the several States." The court concluded that "the Constitution did not give rights and immunities alone, but also imposed responsibilities."[25] The rationale seems to be that when Brown set foot in the state, he carried certain rights with him by force of the Constitution, and those rights carried with them a corresponding duty not to attack the state. His situation was thus quite distinct from that of a foreign army, whose members have no corresponding rights or responsibilities under the U.S. Constitution. Under this theory, mere presence in a state, even in a state of open military hostility, is sufficient to expose one to prosecution under a state's treason laws.

The allegiance issues for two of Brown's black associates were trickier. The attorney for Shields Green, an enslaved man, argued that a "slave could not be guilty of treason" because he was not a citizen. This argument wasn't directly on point, because even noncitizens can owe temporary allegiance. Virginia had executed an enslaved man for treason in 1710 and again in 1778. But in a 1781 case, two dissenting judges argued that slaves were legally incapable of committing treason. A state legislative committee agreed with this conclusion, as did Thomas Jefferson, the state's governor, and the convicted slave was pardoned.[26] The judge in Green's case followed this precedent, and the treason charge was dropped.

John Anthony Copeland, a free black man, was also

charged with treason for his role in Brown's raid. Since he was free, the slavery precedents weren't controlling. And free blacks had been charged with treason against the United States just eight years earlier in the Christiana Riot cases. But Copeland's attorney pointed to the U.S. Supreme Court's notorious 1857 decision in the *Dred Scott* case, which had held that black Americans, whether free or enslaved, were permanently ineligible for American citizenship.[27] One of the primary concerns in Chief Justice Roger Taney's opinion was the Privileges and Immunities Clause—the same clause that had been invoked to justify Brown's prosecution. If free African-Americans were citizens of the United States, they could enter the Southern states and be entitled to all the same privileges and rights as white citizens, a result that Taney viewed as deeply threatening to the stability of slavery.

Copeland's attorney cleverly realized that this argument could be turned on its head. If the Privileges and Immunities Clause imposed burdens on free blacks in Southern states, such as being subject to treason prosecutions (as the government was claiming), it presumably granted them rights as well, a possibility no Southern court was eager to embrace. The judge was persuaded by this argument, and Copeland's treason charge was dropped.[28]

In July 2019, Donald Trump tweeted that his administration would look into claims that Google had committed treason by working with the Chinese government.[29] As chapter 10 will explain, providing assistance to the Chinese is not treason, so nothing is likely to come of this assertion. But Trump's tweet does raise an interesting question about the scope of treason law—can a corporation be indicted for treason? Suppose an American corporation sent thousands of dollars to the German government during World War II. The corporate officers who arranged the transaction could obviously be charged with treason, but what about the corporation itself?

If we rely solely on older law, the answer is clearly no. William Blackstone's *Commentaries on the Laws of England* stated, "A corporation cannot commit treason, or felony, or other crime, in its corporate capacity, though its members may, in their distinct individual capacities."[30] In 1854, the Supreme Judicial Court of Massachusetts agreed, stating that corporations "cannot be guilty of treason."[31]

But in 1909, the United States Supreme Court squarely rejected Blackstone's notion that corporations were immune from criminal indictment. In *New York Central and Hudson River Railroad Co. v. United States*, the Court held, "It is true that there are some crimes which, in their nature cannot be committed by corporations. But [in many other cases] we see no good reason why corporations may not be held responsible" for the crimes committed by their officers. Over the course of the twentieth century, corporations were indicted for a wide array of crimes.[32]

The Court didn't specify which crimes "in their nature" were unfit for corporate punishment, although some obvious examples would include bigamy and adultery. In many ways, treason seems similar to the financial crimes with which corporations are routinely charged. A corporation chartered in an American state and headquartered in an American city could be plausibly said to owe allegiance to the United States. Or, at least, one might reasonably expect that the privilege of doing business in the United States carries with it the fairly minimal obligation of refraining from aiding our enemies in wartime or levying war against the United States. The Supreme Court has dramatically expanded corporate rights under the Constitution in recent years, ruling for corporations in numerous free speech cases, and even finding rights to assert religious freedom under the federal Religious Freedom Restoration Act.[33] Since the nineteenth century, the term "citizens" in Article III's jurisdictional requirements for the federal courts has been interpreted to include corporations.[34] If corporations can receive all of these benefits under the law, there is a strong argument that they should be equally subject to responsibility.

Our existing statutory framework, however, makes it impossible to indict corporations for treason. The federal treason statute provides that treason be punished by either death *or* imprisonment of "not less than five years" and a fine of "not less than $10,000." Obviously, a corporation can't be put to death. But it can't be imprisoned either, and the current statute does not give judges the discretion of imposing only a fine.

Congress could, of course, change the law, to specify that corporations are subject to American treason law and could be punished with a fine alone. In the event of a prosecution, a court would be faced with the difficult question of constitutionality. The corporation's strongest argument would be that such prosecutions were impermissible under eighteenth-century law, and any expansion of the crime would be in tension with the limiting purposes of Article III. The corporation could also assert that artificial entities cannot be meaningfully said to owe allegiance to any national government, especially if the shareholders include persons from a number of foreign countries. On the other hand, the government could counter that the elements of the offense have not been changed, merely the scope of entities subject to prosecution, and that it would be anomalous to exempt corporations from treason prosecutions while exposing them to prosecution for a whole host of other offenses under American law.

How does allegiance to the United States terminate? Temporary allegiance is relatively straightforward—other than the complications raised in the Joyce case, the person simply leaves the country. But permanent allegiance, as the name suggests, is stickier. It can be shed only by voluntarily renouncing United States citizenship. In 1967, the United States Supreme Court held in *Afroyim v. Rusk* that the government has no unilateral power to strip a person of citizenship without his or her consent.[35]

To validly renounce citizenship, a U.S. citizen must voluntarily undertake one of seven acts specifically identified in a federal statute, such as "making a formal renunciation of nationality before a diplomatic or consular officer of the United States in a foreign state," and do so with the specific intent of relinquishing United States citizenship.[36]

This is a strict test, and simply declaring oneself to no longer be a U.S. citizen, for example, is insufficient.[37]

There are two quirks in the law, though. First, one of the renunciation methods recognized in the federal statute is "entering, or serving in, the armed forces of a foreign state if. . . . such armed forces are engaged in hostilities against the United States."[38] Of course, such acts are also acts of treason. But if a person enters into the armed forces of a hostile foreign state with the specific intent of renouncing United States citizenship, he may well be able to avoid a treason prosecution by claiming he no longer owed allegiance to the United States. This defense has several limitations. It would work only if the person was abroad (within the United States he or she would still be bound by temporary allegiance). It would apply only in those rare cases where the United States is engaged in hostilities with a foreign state (and not, say, with a terrorist group). And it would apply only to joining the enemy's army, and not to actions such as spying for the enemy or serving as an enemy propagandist.

The second quirk is that the federal statute provides that citizenship can be renounced by "committing any act of treason against . . . the United States . . . if and when he is convicted thereof by a court martial or by a court of competent jurisdiction."[39] This suggests that convicted traitors can be stripped of their citizenship as part of their punishment. The statute is careful to state that the renunciation occurs only at the time of conviction; otherwise defendants could escape by simply arguing that their treasonous act voided their citizenship, and correspondingly, their duty of allegiance. But it is not at all clear that conviction counts as a voluntary renunciation as required by the *Afroyim* decision, and this statutory provision, although not yet tested in a court of law, may well be found to be unconstitutional.

Under the doctrine of temporary allegiance, noncitizens in the United States, with a few minor exceptions, are fully subject to American treason law. The corollary of this principle is that American citizens traveling abroad are equally subject to the treason laws of foreign countries. So just as William Joyce, an American citizen, was convicted of treason against the United Kingdom, so, too, could American citizens be convicted of treason against France or Russia or Saudi Arabia. The old adage of "When in Rome, do as the Romans do" is good advice, not just for finding a decent meal, but for avoiding a treason prosecution as well.

8

The Unlawful Execution of Hipolito Salazar

Surrounded by the snowcapped peaks of the Sangre de Cristo Mountains, the small town of Taos, New Mexico, is one of the America's most gorgeous destinations. Perched in the high desert at nearly seven thousand feet above sea level, the town now caters to a well-heeled tourist crowd, who stroll through over eighty art galleries and dine at restaurants advertising locally sourced organic fare.

The Taos of one hundred and seventy years earlier, however, was very different. The mountains still loomed, of course, but the town's center was a dusty plaza, resonant with the clomps of burros and redolent with the smell of tobacco, which, as one astonished observer noted, was consumed as enthusiastically by the women of the town as by the men.[1] And a visitor who arrived on April 9, 1847, would have witnessed something even more astonishing:

near the plaza, a scaffold had been erected and six men were hanging from the gallows, executed by American authorities following jury trials in what was called the "District Court of the Territory of New Mexico."[2] Five of the men had been convicted of murder. But one, a thirty-nine-year-old man named Hipolito "Polo" Salazar, had been convicted of high treason for levying war against the United States. It's the sort of thing that ought to leave an impression.

Yet if you searched every book and article ever written about American treason law (and I've read most of them), you would not find a single mention of the execution of Polo Salazar. Indeed, not only do treason scholars fail to mention it, they insist that nothing like it has ever occurred. In his seminal book *The Law of Treason in the United States*, James Willard Hurst wrote, "there has been no execution on a federal treason conviction."[3] Prominent Civil War historian William A. Blair claimed that John Brown was "the first person to be executed for treason since the ratification of the Constitution."[4] And I must sadly plead guilty to the same mistake—in a 2017 *Washington Post* article on treason, I wrote, "No person has been executed by the federal government under the Constitution."[5]

Historians of the American Southwest, however, have addressed the Salazar execution in a small handful of books and articles. But none of these historians has noted the significance of the execution in the context of American treason law: Salazar is the only person ever executed by federal authorities for treason against the United States since the adoption of the Constitution. Southwestern history and treason law scholarship have unfortunately been strangers, passing silently in the night.

The blindness of treason scholars to the Salazar trial is especially regrettable, because the story of Polo Salazar is extraordinary. The only person ever executed by the federal government for treason was not an American, but a Mexican, tried, not in the United States, but in the Republic of Mexico. And the federal government later admitted it had made a terrible mistake—Salazar owed no allegiance to the United States and therefore was not subject to American treason law at all. The horrific consequence was that the only treason execution under federal authority rested on a legal error—the government had executed a legally innocent man.

Although often overshadowed in popular memory by New England, the American Southwest is home to some of the most enduring cities in America. The oldest state capital in the United States, for example, is Santa Fe, New Mexico, which was founded by the Spanish in 1610, ten years before the Pilgrims landed at Plymouth, twenty years before the founding of Boston, and seventy-two years before the founding of Philadelphia. Like Santa Fe, Taos was originally a northern outpost of the Spanish Empire. Following Mexican independence from Spain in 1821, it became a key northern town of the Republic of Mexico.

But conflict would soon arise between Mexican post-independence ideals and the reality of American slavery.

In 1829, Mexico abolished slavery, greatly angering the Anglo-American slaveholders in the Mexican territory of Texas. Several years later, the Texans declared their independence from Mexico, creating the independent Republic of Texas and reinstating slavery.[6] In 1845, the United States admitted Texas to the Union as a slave state.

Disagreements over the location of the border between Texas and the United States led to the United States declaring war on Mexico in 1846 under the leadership of President James K. Polk. The war was bitterly controversial. As a Congressman, Abraham Lincoln opposed it, viewing it as founded on fraudulent premises. Lincoln supported a motion condemning Polk for "unnecessarily and unconstitutionally" starting the war. (As a result, Lincoln was denounced as "traitorous" and as a "Benedict Arnold" by political opponents in his home state of Illinois).[7] Ulysses S. Grant, who fought in the war, later described it as "the most unjust ever waged by a stronger against a weaker nation. . . . Even if the annexation [of Texas] could be justified, the manner in which the subsequent war was forced upon Mexico cannot."[8]

American troops soon swarmed into Mexico, eventually taking the capital city of Mexico City. In northern Mexico, American troops under General Stephen Kearny captured the Mexican city of Santa Fe on August 18, 1846, without firing a single shot. The next day, Kearny addressed the people of the city, stating, "We have come amongst you to take possession of New Mexico, which we do in the name of the government of the United States. . . . You are no longer Mexican subjects; you are now become

American citizens, subject only to the laws of the United States. A change of government has taken place in New Mexico and you no longer owe allegiance to the Mexican government."[9] A few days later, Kearny issued a proclamation warning that any person "found in arms, or instigating others against the United States, will be considered as traitors, and treated accordingly."[10]

These were breathtakingly broad statements, and, as later events would show, founded on serious misunderstanding of the law. But, in theory, if Kearny was correct, the residents of New Mexico were now United States citizens who owed allegiance to the United States. And, as such, they could be guilty of treason against it.

Although Kearny initially occupied New Mexico without bloodshed, many New Mexicans refused to accept American authority. In late 1846, an attempted uprising was thwarted in Santa Fe, and 1847 an armed revolt erupted in Taos, killing Charles Bent, Kearny's appointee as governor of the New Mexico Territory, and a number of other Americans in nearby villages. The American military eventually suppressed the Taos revolt, in the process killing at least two hundred people.[11]

A number of New Mexicans who had participated in the revolts, however, had not been killed but captured, and the question then became what to do with them. General Kearny had issued a code of laws, known as the Kearny Code, for what he called "New Mexico, a Territory of the United States," and had established civilian courts that would function in the American manner, including the use of grand juries and trial juries in criminal cases.[12] These courts had jurisdiction over murder cases, and many of the rebels were tried for murder. Although the code made no specific mention of treason, the newly appointed attorney general for the territory, Francis "Frank" Blair, a twenty-six-year-old graduate of Princeton, was determined to prosecute some of the captured rebels for high treason against the United States.

Blair's legal theory rested heavily on General Kearny's declaration that New Mexico was now a territory of the United States and that its inhabitants were now citizens of the United States. Blair asserted that as "United States district attorney" it was his "duty to prosecute all acts of treason committed by the inhabitants of this territory, holding them responsible for all their acts as citizens of the United States."[13]

Blair soon began presenting his treason indictments to grand juries. In Santa Fe, grand juries declined to indict twenty-five men for treason, but indicted four. Of these, only one case, that against Antonio Maria Trujillo, resulted in a conviction.[14] Trujillo had been charged with "levying war against the government of the United States of America" by sending dispatches to encourage armed rebellion against American forces, and he was sentenced to death.[15] The presiding justice stated that Trujillo had acted with "a band of the most traitorous murderers" that had "ever blackened . . . the annals of history." Trujillo's "foul crimes" justified the jury in finding him "guilty of treason against the government under which [he was] a citizen."[16]

But American officials had doubts about the wisdom of executing Trujillo, who was "seventy-five years of age, necessarily infirm, and evidently near the end of his days."[17] The presiding justice and an associate justice of the court, along with most members of the jury, and, most significantly, prosecuting attorney Frank Blair, all signed a petition for clemency, which was forwarded to officials in Washington, DC.[18] President Polk agreed that a pardon was appropriate, but concluded that pardoning authority rested with the military commander in New Mexico, who appears to have issued the pardon.[19]

The trials at Taos would turn out quite differently. Although Blair had initially sought to try over fifty men for treason, only five were ultimately indicted. Blair declined to pursue three of the cases, and one defendant was acquitted. Only one, Hipolito Salazar, was convicted and sentenced to death. The execution date was set for April 9, 1847. Five other Mexicans, who had been convicted of murder for their role in the revolt, had been sentenced to die on the same day.[20]

But unlike in Trujillo's case, no judge, juror, or prosecutor stepped forward to argue for a pardon, or even for a delay of execution. As the grim day approached, Salazar must have wondered how he could possibly have found himself convicted (at a trial conducted in English, a language he didn't speak) on a charge of treason against the United States (a country that, by his lights, he had never even set foot in).

Salazar's conviction could be justified only if he owed allegiance to the United States. Blair's theory was that

Salazar became a citizen of the United States by virtue of Kearny's proclamation. But this raised a very big question: Could one side in a war between two nations simply declare that the citizens of the other side were now its own citizens, subject to the law of treason for fighting against it?

This objection was repeatedly raised in the New Mexico treason trials from the very beginning. In January 1847, the military had convened a court-martial to try Manuel Chaves, a former Mexican military officer, for treason against the United States. Chaves was defended by William Z. Angney, a captain in the American army, who argued that as Chaves "was not a citizen of the United States there could be no treasonable act on his part, and that in being ready to resist the Americans who had taken possession of the country, was an exhibition of patriotism on his part and worthy of the admiration of all brave men." The United States, Captain Angney warned, "would forever bear the stain of disgrace if it undertook, under any pretext, to shoot a man for endeavoring to defend his country in time of need."[21] The argument was effective, and Chaves was acquitted.

Attorneys for defendants in later trials repeatedly pressed the same objection. In Trujillo's case, the defense argued it was "unconstitutional to try any *native* inhabitant of New Mexico for the crime of treason against the government of the United States, until by actual treaty with Mexico he became a citizen."[22] As one disgusted observer of the Salazar trial noted, "It certainly did appear to be a great assumption on the part of the Americans to conquer a country, and then arraign the revolting inhabitants for treason. . . . Treason, indeed! What did the poor devil know about his new allegiance? . . . I left the room sick at heart." It was a "distorted meaning" of justice to murder those "who defend to the last their country and their homes."[23]

An observer of the Santa Fe trials, in an anonymous letter later published in a prominent Baltimore newspaper, complained about the "farcical" proceedings initiated by Frank Blair, who "prosecutes in the court here individuals who were never citizens of the United States—for the crime of *treason against the United States!*" Under such a theory, the observer noted, the United States could invade the Kamchatka Peninsula and then convict the inhabitants "of treason against the United States, if they speak of revolt against the authority you have forced upon them." Any such trials, like those in Santa Fe, would be "illegal and unconstitutional."[24]

As news of the activities of the American military commanders in New Mexico slowly trickled into Washington, DC, members of Congress and Polk administration officials began to express concerns about the legal justifications for the commanders' actions. In December 1846, a Congressman had warned against "subjecting all the inhabitants of an extensive country to the punishment of treason who should refuse a peaceable submission to our government." Any such action would be "in direct contradiction to all that could be found on the recorded pages of the history of civilized man."[25] Administration officials agreed. In January 1847, Secretary of War William L.

Marcy had warned General Kearny that his code of laws went "beyond the line designated by the President" and that the general had no authority "to confer upon the people of that territory political rights under the Constitution of the United States. . . . The territory in our military occupation, acquired from the enemy by our arms, cannot be regarded, the war still continuing, as permanently annexed to the United States."[26]

In the summer of 1847, Marcy learned not only that this advice had largely been ignored, but that American officials had been trying residents of New Mexico for the crime of high treason against the United States, on the theory that these men had become American citizens. Marcy now sent a stern letter to the American commander in New Mexico to correct the "mistaken views" that "still prevailed in New Mexico." The "foundation of civil government in New Mexico," Marcy explained, "is not derived directly from the laws and constitutions of the United States, but rests upon the rights acquired by conquest." The "territory conquered by our arms does not become, by the mere act of conquest, a permanent part of the United States; and the inhabitants of such territory are not, to the full extent of the term, citizens of the United States." The treason trials were improperly conducted, because the defendants did not owe allegiance to the United States; accordingly it was inaccurate to describe their offenses as treason against the United States. Blair's prosecutions were in "error, so far as it relates to the description of the offense."[27] Although the attorney general had offered to provide a legal opinion on the issue, Marcy concluded that "the error in the designation of the offence was too clear to admit of doubt, and it is only in cases of doubt that resort can be had to the Attorney General for his opinion."[28]

Marcy's conclusion was almost certainly correct. The territory of New Mexico had been conquered by the United States, but until a treaty of peace was concluded, it had not been legally incorporated into the United States and remained formally part of Mexico. (And, depending on the course of the war, it might have easily returned to Mexican control.) Military commanders had no freestanding power to declare that Mexican citizens were now citizens of the United States; that issue could be resolved only by a treaty ending the war. Nor did they have authority to establish United States district courts exercising the judicial power of the United States; that authority is vested solely in Congress. Moreover, only Congress and the president have the power to incorporate foreign territory into the United States and to determine the citizenship status of the territory's inhabitants.

In 1848, the United States and Mexico agreed to the Treaty of Guadalupe Hidalgo. In addition to resolving the Texas border issue, the treaty cut the Republic of Mexico in half, transferring control of modern New Mexico, Arizona, Colorado, Utah, Nevada, and California from Mexico to the United States. In exchange, the United States agreed to pay Mexico $15 million. Whereas General Kearny had abruptly announced that all New Mexicans were now United States citizens, the treaty took a more measured approach, stipulating that Mexican citizens in the portions of Mexico ceded to the United States could decide whether to retain Mexican citizenship or to become citizens of the United States. It would ultimately be their decision, not a military commander's.[29] Those who became United States citizens would be bound by permanent allegiance to the United States; those who remained Mexican citizens would be bound by temporary allegiance so long as they remained in the United States. With the treaty in place, there could be no legal objection to treason trials of the New Mexican inhabitants. But it did not, and could not, retroactively justify the trials that had taken place prior to its adoption.

This basic legal framework was confirmed by an 1850 United States Supreme Court decision arising out of the Mexican War. The precise issue in *Fleming v. Page* was whether the Mexican port of Tampico, which was under the control of the United States military, was a foreign port for purposes of American tariff laws. The Court concluded that it was, holding that a military commander "may invade the hostile country, and subject it to the sovereignty and the authority of the United States. But his conquests do not enlarge the boundaries of this Union, nor extend the operation of our institutions and laws beyond the limits before assigned to them by the legislative power. . . . While [Mexico] was occupied by our troops, [the troops] were in an enemy's country and not in their own."[30]

A modern analogy can help illustrate the point. In 2003, the United States invaded Iraq and became the de facto government of Iraq. But no one thought the invasion made Iraq part of the United States or that the Iraqis were now citizens of the United States. Any American generals who unilaterally announced that the residents of Baghdad were now American citizens and subject to treason prosecutions for resisting American forces would have been quickly stripped of their commands for incompetence. Yet this is precisely what Kearny and Blair did in New Mexico.

The Polk administration was embarrassed by the treason trials and did nothing to publicize them, but members of Congress eventually learned of them and demanded an explanation in the summer of 1848. In a response, President Polk justified military authority over New Mexico, but grudgingly conceded that the treason trials had been unlawful: "That the offenders deserved the punishment inflicted upon them, there is no reason to doubt; and the error in the proceedings against them consisted in designating and describing their crimes as 'treason against the United States.'"[31] Polk noted that the secretary of war had sent instructions to military commanders to prevent the error from recurring.

Frank Blair, the young attorney who zealously prosecuted the treason cases based on a fundamental misunderstanding of the law, appeared to suffer few consequences for his role in one of the worst miscarriages of justice in the history of the United States. He returned to Missouri, where he had previously practiced law, and was elected to the state legislature. He was elected to Congress in 1856 and again in 1860. When the Civil War broke out, Blair strongly supported the Union and was influential in preventing Missouri, a slave state, from joining the

Confederacy. He became a major-general in the Union Army, and impressed General Grant, who recalled in his *Memoirs* that there was "no man braver than he." In 1868, Blair became the Democratic nominee for vice president of the United States, running on the ticket against Grant and Schuyler Colfax. From 1871 to 1873, Blair served as a United States senator from Missouri. A statue of Blair now stands in the United States Capitol, where he is one of two men selected for this honor from Missouri.[32]

And what about the actual man behind the legal documents, the man hanging from the gallows in the plaza at Taos? Unfortunately, we know very little about the life of Hipolito Salazar. He was born in Taos on October 14, 1817, during the decade-long war for Mexican independence. A few weeks after his sixteenth birthday, he married Maria Polonia Serve, with whom he had three sons. At the time of Salazar's execution, Maria was approximately three months pregnant. Their only daughter, also named Maria, was born six months later. She never met her father and, although she would have known that he had been executed as a traitor to the United States, she probably never knew just how distinctive that status truly was.[33]

The sole surviving account of Salazar's execution gives us a glimpse of an indomitable personality. Salazar, the observer noted, "showed a spirt of martyrdom worthy of the cause for which he died—the liberty of his country; and instead of the cringing, contemptible recantation of the others, his speech was firm asservations of his own innocence, the unjustness of his trial, and the arbitrary conduct of his murderers." His final words could have hardly have been more succinct. "With a scowl, as the cap was pulled over his face, the last words he uttered between his gritting teeth were, 'Caraho, los Americanos!'" Or, in English, "F—— the Americans!"[34]

9

The Case of Jefferson Davis, President of the Confederate States of America

In the early hours of Thursday, May 11, 2017, city workers in New Orleans, Louisiana, wearing masks and heavily guarded by police, removed a 106-year-old statue of Jefferson Davis, the president of the Confederate States of America. New Orleans mayor Mitch Landrieu explained the city's reasoning: "To literally put the Confederacy on a pedestal in some of our most prominent public places is not only an inaccurate reflection of our past, it is an affront to our present, and a bad prescription for our future."[1]

Landrieu recognized what most historians have long understood. The Confederate cause was an act of treason against the United States undertaken for the most reprehensible of reasons: the maintenance of white supremacy and race-based slavery. As Confederate vice president Alexander Stephens explained, "the proper status of the negro in our form of civilization . . . was the immediate cause of the late rupture. . . . Our new government is founded upon . . . the great truth that the negro is not equal to the white man; that slavery—subordination to the superior race—is his natural and normal condition. This, our new government, is the first in the history of the world, based upon this great physical, philosophical, and moral truth."[2]

The common practice of referring to the Confederates as "rebels" rather than "traitors" tends to obscure historical reality. Throughout the war, supporters of the Union denounced the Southern secessionists as traitors, which they clearly were.[3] The Confederate Army and those who supported it were "levying war against the United States" under even the narrowest interpretations of that provision. It was the most widespread act of treason in the history of the United States, with hundreds of thousands of people engaged in open warfare against their own government. A Cincinnati newspaper expressed a common sentiment after Fort Sumter: "Treason must be crushed with the strong arm of this Government, and the majesty of the laws vindicated, if need be, by a million of men, at the point of the bayonet and at the cannon's mouth!"[4] Ulysses S. Grant agreed, concluding in April 1861 that there "are but two parties now, Traitors and Patriots and I want hereafter to be ranked with the latter."[5] An Ohio legislator pointed out that the purpose of the war was to "redress the wrongs and insults to our flag and to punish traitors."[6] Union soldiers heartily sang the "Battle Cry of Freedom," one of the best-selling songs in American history, containing the memorable phrase "down with the traitor, up with the stars."[7]

In theory, every Confederate soldier could have been prosecuted, convicted, and executed for treason, with the possible exception of those soldiers who had been drafted into the army, who might have been able to raise a defense of compulsion. But mass executions were neither likely nor desirable. The consistent English and early American practice with rebellions had been to punish only a handful of high-level leaders, while granting generous pardons to everyone else. During the American Revolution, for example, Thomas McKean, the chief justice of Pennsylvania and a signer of the Declaration of Independence, argued that all Loyalists should eventually be pardoned, with the exception of a handful of wealthy or cruel people, whose estates should be forfeited.[8] Similarly, President Abraham Lincoln urged the nation in his Second Inaugural Address to "bind up the nation's wounds" and to act "with malice toward none"—and this did not include drenching the nation with further blood. Following Lincoln's assassination, his successor, President Andrew Johnson, largely followed this advice, issuing an amnesty proclamation on May 29, 1865, to any former Confederate who swore to uphold the Union.

But the Confederacy's principal leaders presented a different case, and they were deliberately excluded from Johnson's initial proclamation. The South's leading general, Robert E. Lee, was arguably saved by the generous actions of General Ulysses S. Grant at Appomattox. Grant's surrender terms pledged to leave the surrendering officers and enlisted men undisturbed by "United States authority" so long as they observed the laws in force where they resided and did not rejoin the Confederate Army.[9] That left the most prominent Confederate of all, Jefferson Davis, the president of the Confederacy, at the center of the Union crosshairs. Many Northerners clamored for his head, arguing that an execution would provide an appropriate conclusion to the Civil War. A group of women from Northampton, Massachusetts, for example, stated that they were "very anxious that Jeff Davis—that traitor who has already lived too long—should be hung up by the neck. . . . Let him be hung! Is the cry of the daughters of the Bay State."[10] Pennsylvania men proposed to erect an enormous scaffold to hang "Jeff Davis the great American Traitor."[11] The notion had been taken seriously since the beginning of the war. An early version of the popular song "John Brown's Body" promised to "hang Jeff Davis to a tree."[12]

The cries of "traitor" would have rung hollow for most of Jefferson Davis's life. Indeed, if he had died in 1860, he would have been remembered primarily as a loyal and dedicated American. A graduate of West Point, Davis had served with distinction in the Mexican War, incurring a painful foot wound at the Battle of Buena Vista. His first wife was the daughter of Zachary Taylor, who later became president of the United States. He had been a member of the United States House of Representatives, a United States senator from Mississippi, and United States secretary of war under President Franklin Pierce. Sometimes mentioned as a possible presidential candidate, he was an early advocate of a federally sponsored transcontinental railroad and had even received an honorary doctor of laws degree from Bowdoin College in Maine. But when Mississippi seceded from the Union in January 1861, Davis reluctantly resigned his United States Senate seat and returned to his plantation home, where over one hundred enslaved persons toiled for the benefit of Davis and his family. A month later, Davis was elected president of the Confederate States of America.

The Confederate Constitution imposed a six-year term for the presidency, without the possibility of reelection. Davis served as Confederate president throughout the Civil War, which, contrary to all initial expectations, dragged on for four bloody years. On April 3, 1865, Union troops seized Richmond, Virginia, the Confederate capital, hoping to capture Davis. But he had fled the city the previous evening and began a long journey south. His luck finally ran out on May 10, 1865, when he was captured by a Union cavalry force in Irwinville, Georgia, and sent into federal custody at Fortress Monroe, Virginia.

Many Americans had hoped that Jefferson Davis would simply disappear, perhaps escaping to England, like Judah Benjamin, the Confederacy's secretary of state. But Davis's capture presented the country with the momentous question of what to do with him. Opinions were bitterly divided, and the fate of Jefferson Davis would prove to be one of the most contentious issues facing America in the post–Civil War years.

The final decision rested with the administration of President Andrew Johnson. There were a number of possible options. Davis could be pardoned outright, as a gesture of national reconciliation that might help heal the wounds of the Civil War. He could be tried by a military tribunal, possibly for complicity in the Lincoln assassination or for war crimes committed at the notorious Andersonville prison. Or, most plausibly, he could be indicted and tried in a civilian court for treason against the United States.

In speeches during the Civil War, Johnson had insisted that "treason must be made odious." He repeated this claim shortly after assuming office, arguing that "treason against the government of the United States *is* the highest crime that can be committed, and those engaged in it should suffer all its penalties. . . . Traitors must be punished and impoverished."[13]

Johnson's cabinet, however, was unable to reach a consensus on Davis's fate. Each option presented serious complications. A pardon of Davis would be inconsistent with all of Johnson's prior statements and would allow a great villain to escape unpunished. A military trial was of doubtful legality and would have raised suspicions that the government was unfairly stacking the deck against Davis. But indictment and trial for treason in civilian court, seemingly the simplest solution, also posed serious difficulties.

The first problem was the jury system. Although some argued for trying Davis in Pennsylvania on the theory that he had been constructively present at the Battle of

Gettysburg, United States Attorney General James Speed rejected that argument, concluding that Davis had to be tried in the state where his crimes were actually committed.[14] That state was Virginia, so any jury would be drawn from a pool of Virginians. There were various techniques to ensure that the jurors would not be arch-Confederates, but the fundamental problem remained: even one juror sympathetic to the Confederate cause (or subject to social pressures) could force a hung jury and prevent a conviction. Even more concerning, a Southern jury might acquit Davis outright, the worst possible outcome from the federal government's perspective.

The second problem was that if Davis was convicted, the Johnson administration would have to decide whether to pardon him or to execute him. Neither option was especially appealing. A pardon looked like irresolution in the face of clear treason, but an execution risked turning Davis into a Southern martyr, around which Confederate sympathizers could rally for generations.

The third problem involved even deeper questions that went to the heart of what the Civil War had supposedly resolved. As legal historian Cynthia Nicoletti has demonstrated in her superb book, *Secession on Trial: The Treason Prosecution of Jefferson Davis*, Davis had a potential defense to the treason charge. Davis would argue, his lawyers suggested, that he was incapable of committing treason against the United States, because at the time of his alleged treasonous acts, he was a citizen of the Confederate States of America; as such, he owed no allegiance to the United

States of America and was legally incapable of committing treason against it. This argument, of course, could prevail only if the secession of the Confederate states was lawful.

But did states have a constitutional right to secede from the Union? The issue had supposedly been resolved by the Civil War itself, and most constitutional historians tend to agree. It was the case of *Grant v. Lee*, decided in 1865 at Appomattox Courthouse. There was something unsettling, however, about a legal issue being decided entirely on the basis of military force, a resolution seemingly reminiscent of discredited medieval trials by combat. No court had ever squarely addressed the constitutionality of secession, but a treason trial of Jefferson Davis would raise the issue directly. For most Northerners it was simply unthinkable that a court would side with secession, effectively declaring unconstitutional the efforts the North had employed to save the Union. What court would ever say that?

Yet there were Northerners who were fervently hoping for precisely that odd result. In 1866, Jefferson Davis received support from the most unlikely person imaginable—Radical Republican Thaddeus Stevens, who had defended Castner Hanway in 1851. Stevens had devoted his entire life to the antislavery cause and was determined to use federal authority and military force to transform the South into a racially egalitarian society. Those goals would be more difficult to achieve if the South had never legally seceded—the Constitution significantly limited certain types of federal authority over the states. But if the Southern states had lawfully left the Union and had then been defeated in a war of conquest, they could be ruled by military authority as conquered territories with none of the constitutional protections given to states. To further the goals of Radical Reconstruction, Stevens thus offered to represent Davis and to help make the argument that secession was constitutional. Under this view, Davis was not legally a traitor, but the former head of state of a conquered foreign country. Although Davis rejected Stevens's offer, concluding that the argument was not helpful to the cause of the South more generally, theories like Stevens's exposed even more difficulties for the Davis prosecution. The strongest opponents of the South might actually support Davis's acquittal.[15]

The final problem arose from an argument stressed repeatedly by Davis's attorney, Charles O'Conor of New York. During the war, the Union had treated the Confederacy as a belligerent power; that is, it had recognized a state of war between the Union and the Confederacy, and had undertaken actions, such as the naval blockade of the South, that were typically only engaged in by two nations at war. The United States Supreme Court had confirmed the legality of these actions in its 1863 decision in *The Prize Cases*,[16] but O'Conor argued that the recognition of belligerent status implied an inability to apply the domestic criminal law of treason to defeated Confederates. As O'Conor put it, "belligerent acts upon the rebel side performed in the due and orderly prosecution of a recognized civil war are not proper subjects of criminal prosecution during the conflict or after its close."[17] Supporters of the Union strenuously disagreed with this theory and insisted that nothing in *The Prize Cases* was intended to preclude subsequent treason prosecutions, but the issue remained open and potentially subject to an adverse ruling in court.[18]

All of these concerns led the federal government to drag its feet. On January 6, 1866, United States Attorney General James Speed issued an opinion stating that when the courts reopened, Davis would be subject to trial for treason in a civilian court in the state where his crimes were committed.[19] But by the end of 1866, no such trial had occurred. In May 1867, after two years in confinement, Davis was transferred to civilian authority and the government consented to his release on bail.

Part of the problem was Chief Justice Salmon P. Chase, who would preside over any trial along with United States District Judge John C. Underwood. Chase had been a prominent supporter of the antislavery cause, and had been a principal rival of Abraham Lincoln for the 1860 presidential nomination. Lincoln appointed Chase as secretary of the treasury and later, following the death of Chief Justice Roger Taney, as chief justice of the United States. Chase had never entirely given up his presidential ambitions and he viewed the prospect of a trial with distaste, fearing that it would undermine his political prospects no matter how it was resolved. Accordingly, Chase relied on a variety of arguments to avoid holding court in Virginia.

In March 1868, the government issued a new treason indictment against Davis to clean up technical problems with the previous indictment. In a vivid demonstration of the changes wrought by the Civil War, the grand jury included three African-Americans and was the first federal grand jury in American history to be racially integrated.[20]

The case looked like it might finally be heading for trial in late 1868, but Chief Justice Chase made a dramatic intervention, tipping off the defense team about a possible new argument that could be made on Davis's behalf.[21] The Fourteenth Amendment, ratified a few months earlier, contained a provision dealing with former Confederate officials. Section Three stated:

> *No person shall be a Senator or Representative in Congress, or elector of President and Vice President, or hold any office, civil or military, under the United States, or under any State, who having previously taken an oath, as a member of Congress, or as an officer of the United States, or as a member of any State legislature, or as an executive or judicial officer of any state, to support the Constitution of the United States, shall have engaged in insurrection or rebellion against the same, or given aid and comfort to the enemies thereof.*

The section's primary effect was to bar most former Confederate officials from holding public office, either in the federal government or the states (although the penalty could be lifted by a two-thirds vote of both houses of Congress). Chief Justice Chase now suggested that Section Three was intended as the exclusive punishment for treason during the Civil War. Because Jefferson Davis was already punished by exclusion from public office, any further prosecution would be unconstitutional.

This argument was not especially compelling, and in normal circumstances might have been dismissed as frivolous. Section Three says nothing about exempting Confederate officials from treason prosecutions or any other criminal punishments. If such a result was intended, the drafters chose a very strange and opaque manner of stating it. As attorney Richard Henry Dana argued on behalf of the prosecution, "Probably nothing would more surprise the people of the United States than to learn that, by adopting Amendment XIV, they had repealed all the penalties against treason, insurrection, or rebellion." Moreover, Davis's interpretation of the amendment led to the "unjust and absurd" result of "reliev[ing] persons holding high office, and therefore the more guilty, from the penalties of death and imprisonment, and leav[ing] those penalties in full force against all persons engaged in a rebellion who did not at the time hold public office."[22]

But Chase seized on this argument like a life preserver—it gave him a face-saving way out of a case that would otherwise hopelessly capsize his political ambitions. When Davis's attorneys moved to dismiss the indictment under the Fourteenth Amendment theory, Chase readily agreed. But the other presiding judge, Judge Underwood, was unpersuaded. With the trial court divided 1–1, the constitutionality of Davis's prosecution was thus set for an appeal to the United States Supreme Court, where, of course, Chief Justice Chase would be one of the justices hearing the appeal.

The bottom line for the Johnson administration, however, was now clear—the chief justice of the United States had stated in open court that the treason prosecution of Jefferson Davis was unconstitutional. On Christmas Day, 1868, President Johnson finally threw in the towel and issued an amnesty proclamation for all Confederates not covered by previous pardons, including Jefferson Davis.

After three and half years of legal jeopardy, Davis was now finally free of the threat of federal prosecution. He learned of his pardon while traveling in Europe and returned to the United States in October 1869. He once again became a president, although this time in the far less exalted position of president of a life insurance company in Memphis, Tennessee. When the company collapsed in the Panic of 1873, Davis explored other business options, none of which proved successful. Eventually, Sarah Dorsey, a wealthy widow in Biloxi, Mississippi, offered Davis a cottage on her estate, known as Beauvoir, where Davis worked on his memoirs. These were finally published in 1881 as a two-volume set, *The Rise and Fall of the Confederate Government*, in which Davis continued to assert the legitimacy of secession, although he downplayed the significance of slavery to the Confederate cause. Davis inherited Beauvoir upon Dorsey's death in 1879, and he continued to live there until his own death in 1889.

Beauvoir remains as the most lasting monument to Jefferson Davis. It opened to tourists in 1941, and although severely damaged in Hurricane Katrina, it has since been restored. Nearby is a newly built Jefferson Davis Presidential Library and Museum.[23] A statue of Jefferson Davis stands outside the library, which was constructed in part with $10 million from the Federal Emergency Management Agency.[24]

If using federal funds to build a library to commemorate Jefferson Davis seems anomalous, an even more striking incongruity can be found in the United States Capitol itself. Each state is allowed to honor two individuals with statues in the capitol; Davis is one of the two honorees from Mississippi, and the only honoree previously indicted for treason against the United States. In a perverse irony, the frozen features of Jefferson Davis thus continue to stare out over the halls of the very government he so ferociously attempted to overthrow.

In 1885, a young Theodore Roosevelt argued in a magazine article that the Civil War was the most important of all modern wars and "also the one in which the dividing lines between right and wrong were sharpest drawn. A Tory of 1776 had far more right on his side than had a Confederate of 1860." Roosevelt also noted that Jefferson Davis "enjoys the unique distinction of being the only American with whose public character that of Benedict Arnold need not fear comparison."[25] Davis responded with a huffy letter to Roosevelt, complaining that the allegation was "libelous and false."[26] But Roosevelt was almost certainly correct. Both Arnold and Davis had indisputably committed treason and both did so after rising to among the highest positions in American government. Davis had been the United States secretary of war, and yet he waged war against his own country, resulting in hundreds of thousands of American deaths. Even Arnold's treason did not have such pernicious consequences. A fair argument can be made that Jefferson Davis was the greatest traitor in American history.

The failure of the Johnson administration to convict Davis of treason, however, has somewhat removed the taint of treason from Davis's historical legacy. Davis is rarely mentioned in the same breath as Benedict Arnold, and indeed to many people the suggestion would seem quite strange. But we are starting to grapple more honestly with the legacy of the Confederacy. As the statues of Jefferson Davis begin to be pulled down across the country, there could not be a better accompaniment than the enduring words of the "Battle Cry of Freedom": "Down with the traitor, and up with the stars."

10

Who Are Enemies of the United States?

There are many forms of betrayal of the United States. Consider just a few hypothetical examples of blatant disloyalty. A United States Congressman is secretly on the payroll of Mexico, and works diligently to advance Mexican interests. A CIA officer reveals sensitive national security secrets to Israel. The secretary of the treasury coordinates all of his actions with Russia, and is treated as a trusted asset by Russian intelligence. A Department of Defense official releases a trove of digital information about our nuclear defenses to a Chinese newspaper, which promptly makes these materials available on the internet.

These cases all sound suspiciously like treason, and most Americans would have little hesitation in labeling the culprits as traitors. In reality, however, none of these actions can be prosecuted as treason against the United States. Cases like these present the most significant tension between the popular understanding of treason and the technical requirements of the law. In all these examples, someone has betrayed the United States—why can't the government prosecute him or her for treason?

The answer turns on the distinctive phrasing of the Treason Clause. Under this provision it is treason to adhere to the "Enemies" of the United States, "giving them Aid and Comfort." The Clause is not concerned with providing aid and comfort to foreign nations generally, or even about placing the interests of another nation ahead of those of the United States. What is prohibited is aid to an "enemy." So what, precisely, is an "enemy"?

As with the "levying war" provision, the term "enemy" in the Treason Clause is borrowed directly from the 1351 English Statute of Treasons and was discussed extensively in English legal treatises of the seventeenth and eighteenth centuries. These definitions have carried over into American law. There are fewer judicial decisions addressing this topic than there are with respect to levying war, but the contours of the law are sharper and easier to discern.

The Treason Clause carefully distinguishes between levying war and aiding enemies, because each defines a distinctive form of treason. The levying war provision looks inward, to internal rebellions. Persons who owe allegiance to the United States and rebel against it are not enemies, but traitors subject to prosecution for levying war. By contrast, the enemies provision looks outward; an enemy is always a foreign state, group, or person who owes no allegiance to the United States. Supreme Court Justice Stephen Field explained it this way during the Civil War: "The term 'enemies' . . . according to its settled meaning, at the time the constitution was adopted, applies only to the subjects of a foreign power in a state of open hostility with us. It does not embrace rebels in insurrection against their own government. An enemy is always the subject of a foreign power who owes no allegiance to our government or country."[1] The offense of adhering to the enemy therefore requires, at minimum, that someone owing allegiance to the United States provides aid and comfort to some entity that does not owe allegiance to the United States.

This fundamental distinction allows us to quickly dismiss a variety of potential claims of treason. If the alleged "enemy" owes allegiance to the United States, there is no treason. Thus, it is not treason to provide aid to the Ku Klux Klan, to the Mafia, to the Crips street gang, to the Westboro Baptist Church, to the American Communist Party, or to any other domestic group that is viewed as somehow threatening to American life. As a matter of law these groups cannot be enemies for purposes of the Treason Clause.

But just being a foreigner is not enough to qualify as an enemy. Most foreign nations and groups are not enemies of the United States at all. An enemy under the Treason Clause only exists if there is a declaration of war between the United States and a foreign nation, open hostilities between the United States and a foreign nation, or open hostilities between the United States and a foreign person or group. Failure to understand this point contributes to the most significant misapprehensions of American treason law.

We can start with nations. The easiest, and rarest, cases involve a formal declaration of war by the United States Congress. Only five wars have been formally declared under the United States Constitution: the War of 1812, the Mexican-American War, the Spanish-American War, World War I, and World War II. All the convictions under the Constitution for adhering to the enemy have come in one of these wars. In each case, the countries against which we declared war were enemies from the moment of the declaration of war until the final conclusion of peace, and the provision of aid and comfort to them constituted treason. But assistance prior to the declaration of war was not. As a 1919 federal court decision explained, Germany became an enemy in World War I only after the declaration of war on April 6, 1917. A German agent in the United States in 1916, even if he "came here for a sinister purpose," was not an enemy. "As we were not at war," the court concluded, "there could under the law be no treason . . . until after the 6th day of April."[2]

Of course, the United States has been involved in far more than five military conflicts. The Vietnam War, for example, was no less a war for being undeclared. English and American courts accordingly recognized that a declaration of war was not an absolute requirement; if there was an actual state of open war between two countries, declared or not, the other country was an enemy. As a prominent English treatise put it, "States in actual hostility with us, though no war be solemnly declared, are enemies within the meaning of the [Treason] Act."[3]

Examining actual hostilities between nations provides many more opportunities to identify enemies. As early as 1798, United States Attorney General Charles Lee concluded that an actual maritime war existed between the United States and France. In an official legal opinion, Lee announced that "France is our enemy; and to aid, assist, and abet that nation in her maritime warfare, will be treason in a citizen or any other person within the United States not commissioned under France."[4] Similarly, the Barbary States, attacked by the Thomas Jefferson administration in the early 1800s, were enemies. More recent enemies include the North Koreans, the North Vietnamese and the Vietcong during the Korean and Vietnam Wars, the Taliban government of Afghanistan, and the government of Iraq under Saddam Hussein.[5]

But in the absence of actual warfare, a foreign nation, no matter how hostile to American interests, is simply not an enemy within the meaning of the Treason Clause. As a federal court explained in 1919, the offense of adhering to the enemy "only takes place, and only can take place, during war—when war is on."[6] This rule explains why none of the examples given at the beginning of this chapter amount to treason. They describe aid to Mexico, Israel, Russia, and China. The United States has not declared war against any of those countries, nor are there open hostilities between the United States and any of them. Accordingly, even the most extensive aid to these nations does not constitute treason.[7]

When the allegations of connections between Donald Trump and Russia began surfacing, I began to receive regular calls from the media inquiring whether or not this conduct was treasonous. As I am no fan of Donald Trump, I would have loved to have said yes. But as a lawyer and a scholar, I knew that the answer was clearly no. Russia is not formally an enemy of the United States. Donald Trump could sell Russia an American aircraft carrier for $10; he could wire the Oval Office with a direct bug to the Kremlin; he could even hand over our nuclear codes to Vladimir Putin, without running afoul of American treason law. Such conduct would clearly warrant impeachment, and would almost certainly violate other provisions of federal law, but it would not amount to providing aid and comfort to the enemy because of the simple fact that Russia is not technically an enemy.

Consider a historical analogy. In the early 1950s, during an especially dangerous phase of the Cold War, Julius and Ethel Rosenberg were accused of transmitting American nuclear secrets to the Soviet Union. The fairness of their trial has been the subject of considerable debate, but later research on their case in American and Soviet archives leaves little question as to their guilt.[8] A casual observer of the trial might easily have concluded that the Rosenbergs were on trial for treason. In his opening statement, federal prosecutor Irving Saypol referred to the "treasonable acts" of the defendants and stated that they had "committed the most serious crime which can be committed against the people of this country."[9] Similarly, in his closing argument, he denounced the defendants as "traitors."[10] Even the presiding judge, Irving Kaufman, adopted this language. When sentencing the Rosenbergs to death, Kaufman stated that their crime was "worse than murder. . . . [P]utting into the hands of the Russians the A-bomb years before our best scientists predicted Russia would perfect the bomb has already caused, in my opinion, the Communist aggression in Korea, with the resultant casualties exceeding 50,000 and who knows but that millions more of innocent people may pay the price of your treason."[11]

But this was pure rhetoric. As Saypol and Kaufman well knew, the Rosenbergs were not on trial for treason—they were charged with conspiracy to commit espionage. Because as despicable as their behavior was (and, from the American perspective, hastening the growth of the Soviet nuclear program is about as despicable as it gets), the Soviet Union was not an enemy of the United States. It had been our ally just a few years earlier during World War II, and although the relationship had deteriorated dramatically, there was no declaration of war or even open hostilities. No matter how great a threat the Soviet Union appeared to pose, it was not treason to aid the Soviet Union.

A more recent example is the case of Aldrich Ames, the high-ranking CIA official who spied for the Soviets for eight years before his arrest in 1994. Ames's betrayal remains the most notorious and damaging failure in the history of the American intelligence services. By any colloquial definition of the term, Ames was a traitor, one of the very worst people America has ever produced. But like the Rosenbergs, Ames could not be tried for treason, because of the simple fact that we were not in a state of open war with the Soviet Union. Ames was charged with espionage and, after pleading guilty, is currently serving a life sentence in a federal prison.[12] If neither the Rosenbergs in the early 1950s nor Aldrich Ames in the 1990s could be prosecuted for treason for aiding the Soviet Union, it is equally impossible to prosecute Donald Trump or anyone else who feels inclined to assist Russia today.

Many Americans are understandably frustrated with the narrowness of this definition. In July 2017, after the revelations of the meeting at Trump Tower between Donald Trump Jr. and a Russian agent, the *Washington Post* asked me to contribute an op-ed about the applicability of treason law to this case. This was a fairly simple task, given the clarity of the law. The *Post* published the op-ed under the headline "Sorry, Donald Trump Jr. Is Not a Traitor."[13] Although the headline aptly summarized the argument that Trump Jr. was not technically guilty of treason, it missed some of the nuance I hoped to convey. I argued that "coordinating with a foreign government to interfere in American elections is fundamentally wrong, deeply un-American, and . . . almost certainly illegal under a variety of federal statutes." I also pointed out that "we do not have a good term to describe behavior that is not technically treasonous but nonetheless constitutes a betrayal of the United States," which was a fair description of Trump Jr.'s alleged activities.

Any such subtleties were lost in the hundreds of comments that followed from angry readers denouncing me for my obvious stupidity, partisanship, and seeming disloyalty to the United States. The comments seemed to proceed from the assumption that it must be treason to work with a foreign country to harm the United States. In many countries it would be. But that is simply not the standard under American law.

Casual allegations of treason are probably inevitable in public discussion of Donald Trump and Russia, and there is little point in countering all of them. But it is surprising to see an esteemed publication such as the *New Yorker* asserting, as it recently did, that allegations of Russian assistance to the Trump campaign "could constitute treason if they were only partly true."[14] Somehow this flatly erroneous claim escaped the *New Yorker*'s renowned and meticulous fact-checkers. It probably seemed so transparently obvious that no fact-checking was necessary. But intuitions about treason are frequently unreliable, and this is especially true with claims about aiding the enemy.

Enemies" are not limited to nations. Under English law, enemies included rogue groups of individuals who were engaged in hostilities with England. The classic example was a foreigner who attacked England on his own initiative, notwithstanding peaceful relations between his country and England. The prominent eighteenth-century treatise of Michael Foster explained, "[I]f the subject of a foreign prince in amity with us invadeth the kingdom without commission from his sovereign, he is an enemy."[15] Similarly, William Blackstone stated that "foreign pirates or robbers, who may happen to invade our coasts, without any open hostilities between their nation and our own" are properly classified as enemies for purposes of treason law.[16] This definition seems to have been readily accepted in America. In the late 1770s, for example, Chief Justice Thomas McKean of Pennsylvania, a signer of the Declaration of Independence (and thus a traitor to Great Britain himself), followed Foster's definition of "enemy" almost verbatim when interpreting the term in his state's new treason law.[17]

The most obvious enemy under this definition is Al-Qaeda, a foreign group that has attacked the United States and with whom the United States is in open hostilities. Al-Qaeda seems directly analogous to the "pirates and robbers" that Blackstone recognized as "enemies" under English treason law. Shortly after 9/11, Congress passed an act authorizing the president "to use all necessary and appropriate force against those nations, organizations, or persons he determines planned, authorized, committed, or aided the terrorist attacks that occurred on September 11, 2001, or harbored such organizations or persons."[18] With this statement, Congress clearly authorized a state of war between the United States and Al-Qaeda. In 2006, the Department of Justice explicitly recognized that Al-Qaeda was an enemy by indicting an American citizen, Adam Gadahn, for treason for providing aid and comfort to Al-Qaeda.[19] A federal court in New York agreed in 2013, concluding that a U.S. citizen who was a member of Al-Qaeda had committed "treason" by giving "aid and comfort to enemies of the United States (such as Al-Qaeda)."[20]

A strong case can also be made that ISIL is an enemy

of the United States under the Treason Clause. Although ISIL is not a nation, and there has been no formal declaration of war (or a declaration equivalent to that against Al-Qaeda), we are clearly in a state of open military hostility against ISIL. In April 2016, for example, President Obama repeatedly stated that our goal was to "destroy ISIL" militarily, and pointed to the fact that the U.S. had launched over 11,500 air strikes against ISIL.[21] Under these circumstances, it would be very hard to argue that a state of open war did not exist between the United States and ISIL.

Although American citizens will undoubtedly have conflicting views as to which foreign nations or groups should count as enemies, final resolution rests with the federal government. Only the United States Department of Justice can initiate prosecutions for treason against the United States, and the department will do so only after serious consultation with other federal departments. After all, declaring a nation or group an "enemy" for purposes of the Treason Clause is tantamount to a declaration of war and will only be undertaken in the most serious of circumstances.

Federal courts have a role to play in these cases, but it is relatively limited. As a general matter, determinations of a state of war are quintessential "political questions," meaning that their resolution is entrusted to the legislative and executive branches of government. Courts have little ability to second-guess the federal government's determination that a foreign nation or group is an enemy. But courts still must carefully evaluate any treason indictment to ensure that it meets the minimum constitutional requirements. A court would clearly dismiss a treason indictment, for example, if the asserted "enemy" was the Democratic Party or the Sierra Club or the *Chicago Tribune*.[22]

Moreover, courts must ensure that the government's "enemy" determination is backed up by other previous, publicly available statements. As a matter of fundamental due process, and implicit in the concept of "*open* warfare," is the requirement that a person have notice that the government considers a nation or group to be an enemy. The government cannot secretly declare a country to be an enemy, and then punish those people who interact with it. As one federal court has explained, "there must be some determination by the political department of the government evidencing the existence of a state of war."[23] This is a further problem with treating Russia as an enemy—there are no official actions of the United States government indicating that we are in a state of open war with Russia.

A hypothetical analogy can help illustrate the point. Suppose that in 2016 the Canadian government was appalled by the prospect of Donald Trump assuming power on its southern border. Prime Minister Justin Trudeau then sent undercover agents into Michigan, Wisconsin, and Minnesota to distribute handbills promoting the election of Hillary Clinton. No one would seriously think that this secret conduct amounted to a state of open war between the United States and Canada, or that aid to the

Canadian government now constituted treason against the United States. But the Canadian hypothetical is simply the analogue equivalent of the documented digital behavior of Russia.[24]

Of course, Russian meddling in our elections is an outrage and a despicable act of hostility by a foreign government. Indeed, the United States might even be justified in treating such Russian meddling as an act of war and taking military action against Russia in response.[25] But this would be one of the most significant decisions our country could possibly make, likely leading to a global war with immense consequences for humanity. So we will almost certainly have to deal with Russia by other means. And so long as we do not recognize a state of open war with Russia, that country remains what we might call a "frenemy"—hostile, dangerous, and adverse to American interests but, technically, still a friend.

There is one final way in which seemingly obvious intuitions about treason and the enemy are not to be trusted. Suppose an American citizen traveled to Tokyo in September 1941 and encouraged the imperial Japanese government to attack the United States. After the attack, could the American citizen be charged with treason?

The answer, astonishingly, is probably no. This bizarre result rests on a subtle distinction between English and American treason law. In 1762, Michael Foster summarized the English law on this point, stating:

> *The offence of inciting foreigners to invade the kingdom is a treason of signal enormity. In the lowest estimation of things and in all possible events, it is an attempt, on the part of the offender, to render his country the seat of blood and desolation; and yet,* unless the powers so incited happen to be actually at war with us at the time of such incitement, the offence will not fall within any branch of the statute of treasons, *except that of compassing the king's death.*[26] [Emphasis added.]

In other words, until the surprise attack is actually launched, the other country is technically not an enemy, whatever its secret, hostile intentions might be. Accordingly, persuading another country to attack England could not be prosecuted as an act of adhering to the king's enemies. Foster concluded, however, that such persuasion could be punished under an entirely different provision of English treason law—the prohibition on compassing the death of the king.

The drafters of the Treason Clause wrote against this backdrop of English law. But they deliberately eliminated the offense of compassing the king's death, and they did not adopt anything of analogous scope. The curious consequence is that a particularly nasty form of disloyalty—persuading a foreign country to attack us—may escape punishment as treason. Since it technically doesn't count as levying war or adhering to enemies, it could only be punished under some other criminal statute. However, if the American participated directly in the Pearl Harbor attack, say, by flying a plane, he could probably be charged with levying war against the United States.[27]

In short, under American treason law, many forms of blatant disloyalty cannot be punished as providing aid and comfort to the enemy. Fortunately, law enforcement is not limited to the crime of treason when hunting down malefactors. The Rosenbergs were not technically convicted of treason, but that fact probably didn't provide them much comfort as they were being strapped into the electric chair. Eighteenth-century English law provided that aid to a foreign country with whom England was not at war could be punished as a felony, although not as treason.[28] American law has followed this distinction. Laws regarding espionage, conspiracy, the treatment of classified materials, the conduct of political campaigns, laundering money, making false statements to the FBI, providing material support to terrorist organizations, and a host of other provisions all provide the government with considerable tools for prosecuting and convicting people who act in a disloyal manner. And these laws can be easily updated to capture disloyal conduct that might currently fall through the cracks. We may be denied the satisfaction of formally labeling certain disloyal Americans as traitors, but that doesn't mean they will escape scot-free.

11

Tokyo Rose and the World War II Radio Broadcasters

In 1920, the first commercial radio station opened in Pittsburgh, Pennsylvania.[1] Over the next twenty years, the radio business boomed, bringing the world together across previously unimaginable distances. Like all new technologies, it was quickly adapted for military purposes.[2] Governments realized that radio could be used not only for troop communications but also for safely broadcasting propaganda directly into the heart of enemy territory. Radio broadcasts to wide audiences, which were nonexistent during World War I, took on enormous significance in World War II. The government of Nazi Germany, for example, viewed radio propaganda as a vital part of its war effort. As one Nazi propagandist later testified, German broadcasts aimed at American listeners were intended "to build up racial controversies, to create unrest regarding the economic inequalities in the country . . . . [to drive] a wedge between the people and the Roosevelt Administration, and [possibily get] a government elected in the United States which would be against interference in European affairs."[3]

Effective propaganda, of course, required fluency in the listener's own language, so native speakers were essential. In the Pacific Ocean, American service members listened to broadcasts from Radio Tokyo, where English-speaking broadcasters presented programs of popular music and occasional Japanese propaganda. The Americans called the female broadcasters "Tokyo Rose." In Europe, "Axis Sally" (in reality an American citizen named Mildred Gillars) broadcast propaganda from Nazi Germany. So did the American journalists Douglas Chandler and Robert H. Best. And in Italy, the American poet Ezra Pound conducted propaganda broadcasts on behalf of Mussolini's fascist government.

All of these Americans would eventually be charged with treason for their broadcasting activities. These cases brought a modern twist to the old charge of aiding the enemy. The defendants did not provide military supplies or financial assistance. Instead, they were charged with sitting in a small room, projecting their voices over invisible radio waves in the direction of American troops.

The most legendary of these broadcasters was "Tokyo Rose." Popular accounts insisted that a Japanese-American woman named Iva Toguri D'Aquino was the one and only

"Tokyo Rose." In 1949 Toguri was tried and convicted of treason against the United States, and for many Americans her guilt seemed firmly established. Even today, the name "Tokyo Rose" is almost synonymous with traitor. But Toguri's journey from obscurity to infamy reveals a far more complicated story, one of a young woman who may not have betrayed her country at all.

Nothing about Iva Toguri's childhood in Southern California suggested that she would someday find herself charged with treason against the United States. She was born in Los Angeles on the Fourth of July, 1916, to parents who had emigrated from Japan. Although her parents were barred from American citizenship by the race-based restrictions then in force, Toguri was an American citizen by birth. In many ways, her childhood was thoroughly assimilated into the American mainstream—English was the primary language in her home, the family attended a Methodist church, she played tennis and was a member of the Girl Scouts, and most of her acquaintances were white.[4] As one scholar notes, "in order to become a genuine and true American," she "seemed to have come to despise everything Japanese, including Japanese foods, especially rice."[5] She attended UCLA, where she was a member of an Asian-American sorority, and graduated in 1940 with a degree in zoology.[6]

In June 1941, the Toguri family received a fateful letter. Iva Toguri's aunt, her mother's twin sister, was mortally ill in Japan. Although Iva's mother was herself too sick to make the journey, the family decided to send Iva instead. On July 5, 1941, Iva Toguri departed the United States en route to Yokohama. When she arrived, she discovered that she didn't particularly like Japan, and she was eager to return home in the fall of 1941. But her efforts were hindered by deteriorating relations between the United States and Japan and bureaucratic obstacles arising from her lack of a United States passport. The attack on Pearl Harbor on December 7, 1941, foreclosed the return journey entirely. Toguri was now stuck behind enemy lines, in a country whose language she did not speak and whose culture she only partially understood.[7]

Desperate for a job, Toguri began working for the Dōmei News Agency, roughly the Japanese equivalent of the Associated Press, as a transcriber of English-language broadcasts.[8] Japanese officials encouraged Toguri to renounce her American citizenship and become a citizen of Japan, but she refused to do so.[9] Meanwhile, her family back in the United States was sent to an internment camp.

In August 1943, Toguri took a second job as an English-language typist for Radio Tokyo. Later that fall, she was recruited by several Allied POWs who had been forced to broadcast for the Japanese. They hosted an English-language program called "Zero Hour," which was targeted at American service members in the Pacific. The POWs deliberately tried to sabotage the Japanese propaganda efforts, and they believed Toguri could be trusted to help them. Toguri began broadcasting on "Zero Hour" and identified herself as "Orphan Anne." The broadcasts, which primarily involved introducing musical selections, continued until the end of the war and were enormously popular with American service members.[10] Charles Cousens, the Australian POW who wrote most of the scripts, later testified that he "tried to make a complete burlesque of the program." Rather than the "feminine seductive voice" that soldiers later attributed to Tokyo Rose, Toguri had a "rough, almost masculine" voice, a "comedy voice" that Cousens "needed for this particular job."[11]

The much-discussed "Tokyo Rose" was an imagined amalgam of many people. No announcer on Radio Tokyo ever identified herself as "Tokyo Rose," and at least five other English-speaking women served as announcers on Radio Tokyo during the war.[12] Indeed, Frederick P. Close has argued that "Tokyo Rose" was a legend created out of the fertile imaginations of American servicemen. The name appeared in military reports as early as March 1942, when Radio Tokyo had featured only one woman broadcaster for less than an hour. The legend grew, until she was attributed with almost total omniscience. "Tokyo Rose" supposedly broadcast details about troop movements and military secrets, the names and ranks of individual service members, and even the names of their girlfriends. But none of this was true—no Radio Tokyo broadcast included such details, to which the Japanese did not have access.[13] An army intelligence report complained that "countless unfounded rumors" about "Tokyo Rose" were "great headaches" and a form of "unwitting propaganda originated by our own forces."[14]

The enormous public significance accorded to "Tokyo Rose," however, led to intense efforts to identify her at the end of the war. After the Japanese surrender, journalists rushed to Tokyo in an attempt to land the ultimate scoop. A pair of Hearst reporters managed to locate Iva Toguri, and she agreed to give them an exclusive interview for $2,000 (nearly $30,000 in today's money). In a contract, she foolishly and falsely stated that she was "the one and original 'Tokyo Rose' who broadcast from Radio Tokyo" and she had "no feminine assistants or substitutes." She even signed the contract as "Iva Ikuko Toguri (Tokyo Rose)."[15] Not surprisingly, this publicity effort blew up in her face. Toguri was arrested by military officials for treason against the United States and spent over a year in custody in Japan.[16]

After careful study of her case, however, the Department of Justice concluded that Toguri had not committed treason. She had only introduced musical selections and broadcast "nothing whatever of propaganda, troop movements or any further attempts to break down the morale of the American forces."[17] Her broadcasts, a Justice Department lawyer concluded, "were innocuous and could not be considered giving aid and comfort to the enemy."[18] A 1948 review of the case by Thomas DeWolfe, the Justice Department's top treason expert, reached the same conclusion, finding that Toguri's broadcasts were "totally innocuous" and that the government could not prove any disloyal intent. Any prosecution, DeWolfe argued, would likely result in a directed verdict for the defense.[19]

The Justice Department's recommendations were informed by substantial experience with treason cases arising out of World War II radio propaganda. In June 1947, the department had prosecuted Douglas Chandler for broadcasting from Nazi Germany. A journalist and a United States citizen, Chandler was viciously anti-Semitic and a firm believer in the Nazi cause. He traveled to Berlin in February 1941, where he volunteered his services to the propaganda ministry, headed by Joseph Goebbels. When Germany declared war on the United States, Chandler voluntarily chose to remain in Germany, continuing to work as a highly paid employee of the German Radio Broadcasting Company. At his trial, the Justice Department introduced twelve recordings of Chandler's broadcasts into evidence, and presented a dozen witnesses who testified to their personal knowledge of his work at the radio station. The defense never denied that Chandler made the recordings or that he was a Nazi adherent; instead, it attempted an unsuccessful insanity defense. The jury easily convicted Chandler of ten overt acts of treason, and the judge sentenced him to life in prison.[20]

Similarly, American journalist Robert H. Best had been convicted of treason in the spring of 1948. Best was in Vienna at the time of the Pearl Harbor attack, and was scheduled to be returned to the United States. He refused this offer, however, and went to Berlin, where, like Chandler, he began broadcasting propaganda for the German Radio Broadcasting Company. For Best, "Hitler's crusade" was a "sacred cause," and he sought to maximize the effectiveness of German propaganda. Prosecutors introduced seven recordings of Best's broadcasts, which warned of a Jewish worldwide conspiracy and praised Hitler's Germany. The jury convicted Best on the twelve counts that were submitted to it, and, like Chandler, he was sentenced to life imprisonment.[21]

The government was also preparing to prosecute Mildred Gillars, colloquially known as the infamous "Axis Sally."[22] An American actress who moved to Germany in 1934, Gillars was a virulent anti-Semite, and from May 1940 to May 1945, she broadcast Nazi propaganda on German radio. Typical statements included: "damn Roosevelt, damn Churchill and damn all of their Jews who have made this war possible"; "the Jews are sending our men over to Europe to fight so that their money bags will get filled"; "I ask you American women if you brought your boys up to be murderers? Have you? Because that's what they're becoming"; "Germany has vision. Germany has culture. Germany has supplied all of Europe, to say nothing of America and other western countries with culture. I ask you Americans, 'What have you done for posterity?'"; "I'd rather die for Germany than live one hundred years on milk and honey in the Jewish America of today."[23] She was eventually convicted in March 1949 for participating in the broadcast "Vision of Invasion," a propaganda effort to counter the projected Allied invasion of Europe by depicting a dead American soldier appearing in a dream to his mother. The government not only introduced a recording of the broadcast, it had three witnesses to Gillars's participation. Gillars was sentenced to ten to thirty years in prison and a $10,000 fine.[24]

The Justice Department had also worked to build a treason case against the distinguished American poet Ezra

Pound. From 1941 to 1943, Pound had broadcast pro-fascist propaganda on Italian radio. The broadcasts, which were so incoherent the Italians suspected they might be coded messages, are perhaps best described as rants; the most consistent theme was a raging anti-Semitism, coupled with denunciations of Allied leaders and claims that the United States should not be in the war.[25] In one broadcast, for example, Pound claimed, "I think it might be a good thing to hang Roosevelt and a few hundred yidds IF you can do it by due legal process."[26] In another, he argued that the "reasons for both England and America being in the war are dishonest, basically and fundamentally dishonest."[27]

On account of these broadcasts, Pound was indicted by a federal grand jury in 1943 on a charge of treason. Arrested in Italy in 1945 by American military forces, Pound was brought to Washington, DC, for trial. Two witnesses to the same overt act would not be a problem—the FBI had identified five Italian eyewitnesses who could testify to Pound's broadcasts. A panel of four psychologists, however, found that Pound was mentally incompetent to stand trial, and he was committed to St. Elizabeths Hospital. In April 1958, Pound's lawyers moved to dismiss the indictment, and the United States government did not object. Released after nearly twelve and a half years in St. Elizabeths, Pound returned to Italy, where he died in 1972.[28] Pound was the most famous twentieth-century American to be charged with treason, and if he had been found fit to stand trial, he would likely have been convicted in 1946.[29]

Compared to these cases, the evidence against Iva Toguri was extremely thin. The government had no recordings of Toguri broadcasting propaganda, no evidence that Toguri had expressed support for the Japanese, and no evidence that Toguri had voluntarily stayed in Japan.

Most of the Radio Tokyo broadcast scripts had been destroyed, and listeners who had only heard the broadcasts would have been unable to identify the speaker. Moreover, all accounts indicated that Toguri's broadcasts were innocuous—she had merely introduced musical programs, but had not commented on the war in a traitorous manner. Even the few surviving broadcast recordings and scripts contained no forceful propaganda, like that in the Chandler, Best, and Gillars cases, but merely "a little patter and sassy quips."[30] The surviving scripts even indicate that Toguri regularly joked about spreading "propaganda," which was hardly consistent with a serious propaganda effort.[31] Given all of these problems, it is not surprising that the Justice Department initially declined to prosecute Toguri.

But on August 16, 1948, everything changed. United States Attorney General Tom Clark announced that Toguri (now known as D'Aquino after her April 1945 marriage to Felipe D'Aquino) would be tried for treason in San Francisco. It was a presidential election year, and the Truman administration wanted to show that it was tough on disloyalty.[32] The prosecution would be led by Thomas DeWolfe, despite his previous conclusion that there was no justification for a treason prosecution.

A fundamental problem for the government was the Constitution's requirement of two witnesses to the same overt act. Under the 1945 *Cramer* decision, the overt act had to "show sufficient action by the accused, in its setting, to sustain a finding that the accused actually gave aid and comfort to the enemy."[33] The prosecution managed to find two former Radio Tokyo employees, both American-born Japanese, and potentially subject to treason charges themselves, to testify that Toguri had broadcast the statement, "Now you fellows have lost all your ships. You really are orphans of the Pacific now. How do you think you will ever get home?"[34] In 1976, these witnesses admitted that their testimony was false and that Toguri "never broadcast anything treasonable."[35] But in 1949, their testimony, if believed, would be sufficient to sustain a treason charge in front of a jury.

The government viewed the composition of the jury as critical. The FBI conducted extensive investigations of all 221 people on the jury list, prosecutors used their peremptory challenges to exclude Asian-Americans and African-Americans from the jury, and Toguri ended up facing an all-white jury.[36] A columnist in the *San Francisco Chronicle* denounced the prosecution for racially discriminatory conduct, but in 1949 no legal rule barred the prosecution from acting in the way it did.[37] Not until 1986 would the United States Supreme Court forbid the use of racially discriminatory peremptory challenges by prosecutors.[38]

The trial began in early July 1949 and lasted for twelve weeks. Toguri was represented by Wayne Collins, a San

Francisco lawyer who had previously represented Fred Korematsu in his challenge to the exclusion of Japanese-Americans from the West Coast. Collins waived his fees and defended the case vigorously, but he may not have been well equipped to handle the intricacies of a treason case. The brief he later filed in her appeal, for example, was described by the appellate court as "almost unintelligible."[39]

Most observers of the trial concluded that Toguri was innocent, and the jury initially leaned 11–1 for acquittal.[40] But the jury ultimately reached a compromise verdict; Toguri was acquitted on seven of the eight counts, but convicted on the count of broadcasting the "orphans of the Pacific" comment. This was the most plausible count on which to convict; there were two witnesses who testified to this overt act, and Toguri had seemingly admitted the phrase in a 1945 interview with a reporter. Frederick P. Close, who has written the most extensive analysis of the Toguri case, reluctantly concludes that Toguri probably did broadcast the comment.[41] On the other hand, the evidence was far less compelling (and the alleged statement far less vituperative) than in the other broadcasting cases. Moreover, there was some evidence that Toguri had acted under duress, and it was not clear that she acted with the requisite intent to betray the United States.

The judge sentenced Toguri to ten years in federal prison and imposed a $10,000 fine. Toguri served six years and two months of the sentence at a women's prison in West Virginia, before being released on parole. But with the passage of time, her case began to be reconsidered.

Amid renewed media interest in the trial, the two principal witnesses against her recanted, and in January 1977 Toguri received a full pardon from President Gerald Ford. Although she would never shake the "Tokyo Rose" label completely, Toguri would be largely rehabilitated. In January 2006, Toguri received the Edward J. Herlihy Citizenship Award from the World War II Veterans Committee, an honor that would have been unthinkable in 1949.[42] Eight months later, Toguri died at the age of ninety.

A significant question lingers over the World War II radio broadcasting cases—were the defendants' broadcasts protected by the First Amendment, which guarantees freedom of speech? Under modern law, it is almost impossible to prosecute people for statements of political opinion. In a letter to United States Attorney General Francis Biddle, Ezra Pound wrote, "Free speech under modern conditions becomes a mockery if it do [sic] not include the right of free speech over the radio."[43]

Several of the broadcasting defendants made this argument in court. Their strongest argument was that prior treason cases had suggested that words alone were not treason; there must be some overt act apart from mere words. Here, the defendants had merely expressed unpopular opinions, opinions that in themselves could not constitute treason. Even Attorney General Biddle was initially concerned that this defense would be successful.[44]

It wasn't. Every court that considered the argument rejected it. The most extensive analysis came in Douglas

Chandler's case, where the United States Court of Appeals for the First Circuit agreed that, in general, political opinions cannot be prosecuted: "Thus, a citizen in the exercise of his ordinary political rights may—intemperately as he pleases—criticize the President for getting the country into war, hold up to ridicule the bungling and incompetence with which our civilian and military leaders are conducting the war, express the view that we cannot possibly win the war, and that the thing to do is vote in a new administration which will negotiate peace on the best terms obtainable and save the country from a greater disaster. The speech may tend to weaken our country in its war effort by inducing divided counsels and a spirit of defeatism, and in that sense may be of aid and comfort to the enemy."[45]

But it was absurd, the First Circuit concluded, to extend that proposition to immunize all words from prosecution for treason. A simple, but powerful, example proved the point. A person who conveys military intelligence to the enemy does so with words alone, but his act is clearly treasonous nonetheless.[46] Chandler's case was similar—he had "trafficked with the enemy and as their paid agent collaborated in the execution of a program of psychological warfare designed by the enemy to weaken the power of the United States to wage war successfully." The court concluded, "It is preposterous to talk about freedom of speech in this connection. . . . Trafficking with the enemy, in whatever form, is wholly outside the shelter of the First Amendment."[47]

Although free speech protections have expanded significantly since World War II, the First Circuit's conclusion seems intuitively correct. There is a significant difference between spreading antiwar propaganda internally on one's own volition and doing so as an agent of an enemy nation. The former is part of the free discussion we tolerate in an open and democratic society; the latter is a clear case of giving aid and comfort to the enemy.[48]

The Iva Toguri case is a powerful reminder of the dangers of treating treason prosecutions as political weapons. By overruling its own prior conclusion that Toguri had not committed treason, the Department of Justice sought to bolster the Truman administration's national security credentials in a world increasingly concerned about the Cold War with the Soviet Union. But it took little account of the human cost imposed on a woman who had done almost nothing wrong. The "Tokyo Rose" of legend may have committed treason; the Iva Toguri of reality almost certainly did not.

12

What Is "Adhering to the Enemy, Giving It Aid and Comfort"?

Under Article III, it is treason to adhere to the enemies of the United States, giving them aid and comfort. These phrases were taken directly from the 1351 English Statute of Treasons. But what do they actually mean?

Unfortunately, there is no precise definition of "aid and comfort." In 1919, a federal court concluded that "aid and comfort" included acts that "strengthen or [tend] to strengthen, the enemies of the United States in the conduct of a war against the United States" and acts that "weaken, or tend to weaken, the power of the United States to resist or to attack the enemies of the United States."[1] As a very broad generalization, this is roughly correct, but it cannot be relied upon to resolve actual cases. Consider, for example, a newspaper editorial attacking a proposed tax hike to support a war. Such an editorial may well strengthen the enemy or weaken the United States, but it is entitled to full protection under the Free Speech Clause of the First Amendment and is not an act of treason.

One way to approach the issue is to consider the specific acts that American courts have held to be overt acts of providing aid and comfort to the enemy. Since the adoption of the U.S. Constitution, these include abusing American prisoners of war;[2] broadcasting propaganda for the enemy;[3] sheltering an enemy agent, providing an enemy agent with a car, and helping an enemy agent obtain a job;[4] escorting an enemy agent in a car, escorting an enemy agent to a café, providing food and drink to an enemy agent, and introducing the agent to others under a false identity.[5]

These cases suggest that the aid and comfort must provide some benefit to the enemy that is directly related to the military conflict with the United States. For example, in the "Tokyo Rose" case, simply broadcasting music over Radio Tokyo was seen as insufficient to justify a treason charge. One could argue that the Empire of Japan benefited from this service, either because it freed up another person who could then hold a military job, or because it made Japan appear less threatening to the enemy. But this benefit was simply too indirect—the government had to show that she broadcast propaganda aimed at American troops.

Similarly, in a 1952 case, the U.S. Supreme Court considered the appeal of Tomoya Kawakita, a U.S. citizen who worked as an interpreter at a Japanese nickel factory during World War II. But Kawakita was not charged with treason simply for holding that job. Indeed, the Court suggested it would be absurd to indict an American citizen trapped behind enemy lines simply for accepting employment; a person's need for a livelihood might always "indirectly help the enemy nation." Instead, the treason charge against Kawakita was based on specific acts of cruelty to American prisoners of war working at the factory, such as beating them and kicking them.[6] As the Supreme Court stated, if the act "gives aid and comfort to the enemy at the immediate moment of its performance, it qualifies as an overt act within the constitutional standard of treason." Kawakita's actions "showed more than sympathy with the enemy. . . . They showed conduct which actually promoted the cause of the enemy. They were acts which tended to strengthen the enemy and advance its interests. These acts in their setting would help make all the prisoners fearful, docile, and subservient."[7]

The most extensive analysis of aid and comfort in an American judicial decision came in 1945, when the United States Supreme Court heard an appeal of a treason conviction for the first time. The case began in 1942, when Hitler's government managed to secretly insert eight saboteurs into the United States with a mission to sabotage the American war industry. Two of the Nazi saboteurs, Werner Thiel and Edward Kerling, met up in New York City with Anthony Cramer, a German immigrant who had been naturalized as a United States citizen. Thiel and

Kerling met Cramer in several public places for drinks, and Thiel later gave Cramer a money belt, containing over $3,000, most of which Cramer placed in his own safe-deposit box. The government alleged that Cramer was aware of the saboteurs' nefarious purposes. At trial, the prosecution presented two witnesses to the meetings for drinks. It did not have two witnesses to the money belt, the safe-deposit box, or any other overt act.[8]

The Supreme Court reversed Cramer's conviction by a 5–4 vote. The issue turned on the nature of the overt act requirement. The defendant contended that his drinks with Thiel were on their face innocuous—there was no testimony about the nature of their conversation. Merely having drinks with a suspected enemy agent is not in itself a form of giving aid and comfort to the enemy. In the defense's view, the overt act "alone and on its face must manifest a traitorous intention."[9] The government, by contrast, argued that it need only prove two witnesses to some overt act, using other testimony to establish that the overt act "was a step in treason and was done with treasonable intent."[10]

The majority of the Court was unhappy with either alternative. The defense's view "would place on the overt act the whole burden of establishing a complete treason." But the government's view would permit convictions based on two witnesses testifying to "an apparently commonplace and insignificant act," thus reducing the function of the overt act requirement to "almost zero." The Court attempted to strike a middle ground, although it leaned more closely to the defense's position. In an opinion by

Justice Robert Jackson, the Court held that the overt act must "show sufficient action by the accused, in its setting, to sustain a finding that the accused actually gave aid and comfort to the enemy." Moreover, every "act, movement, deed, and word of the defendant charged to constitute treason must be supported by the testimony of two witnesses." Under this standard, Cramer's conviction could not stand. "It is difficult to perceive any advantage," Jackson wrote, "which this meeting afforded to Thiel and Kerling as enemies or how it strengthened Germany or weakened the United States in any way whatever. . . . Meeting with Cramer in public drinking places to tipple and trifle was no part of the saboteurs' mission and did not advance it. It may well have been a digression which jeopardized its success."[11]

Four justices, led by Justice William O. Douglas, vigorously dissented, arguing that the Court's decision departed from historical precedent and made treason far too difficult to prove. In their view, the primary purpose of the overt act requirement was "to preclude punishment for treasonable plans or schemes or hopes which have never moved out of the realm of thought or speech."[12] Demanding that the overt act in itself be treasonous, Douglas claimed, "makes the way easy for the traitor, does violence to the Constitution, and makes justice truly blind."[13]

Cramer certainly imposes many hurdles on prosecutors. Not only must they find two witnesses to the same overt act, that overt act must directly demonstrate the giving of aid and comfort to the enemy. The prosecution failed in Cramer's case because it lacked two witnesses to his receipt of the money belt and his storage of the money in the safe-deposit box, either of which would have been sufficient acts of providing aid and comfort to the enemy.[14] But treason is often committed in secret, and finding two witnesses can be a significant hurdle.

On the other hand, *Cramer* does not, by any means, make it impossible to prosecute treason cases. The Department of Justice brought nearly a dozen treason cases after *Cramer*, and, as law professor Paul Crane has pointed out, "every treason prosecution brought to trial resulted in a conviction, and every treason conviction but one was affirmed on appeal."[15] Just two years after *Cramer*, the Supreme Court affirmed a treason conviction in another opinion by Justice Jackson. In that case, a different Nazi saboteur had received assistance from his father. The Court held, "there can be no question that sheltering, or helping to buy a car, or helping to get employment is helpful to an enemy agent."[16] And, as noted previously, the Court upheld the treason conviction of Tomoya Kawakita in 1952 for abuse of American prisoners at a POW camp in Japan.[17]

Failed attempts to aid the enemy pose a particularly difficult problem for treason law. Suppose someone mails classified military intelligence to the enemy, but the letter is intercepted by the government and never reaches the intended recipient. One could argue that aid and comfort have not actually been "given." There was an attempt, but it failed, and therefore it cannot be considered an act of treason.

Historically, courts rejected this argument. Michael Foster, in his prominent eighteenth-century treatise on English law, argued that "the bare sending of money or provisions . . . or sending intelligence to . . . enemies, which in most cases is the most effectual aid that can be given them, will make a man a traitor, though the money or intelligence should happen to be intercepted." Although the attempt failed, "the party in sending did all he could—the treason was complete on his part though it had not the effect he intended."[18] In 1863, Justice Stephen Field of the United States Supreme Court, citing Foster, charged a jury that it "is not essential to constitute the giving of aid and comfort that the enterprise commenced should be successful and actually render assistance."[19] The key is that the perpetrator had performed the necessary steps to complete an act of treason—the effort failed only because of intervening events.

This type of failed attempt—where the sending of intelligence was intercepted by a third party—can be distinguished from other types of botched attempts. The classic case is from the American Revolution, when an American named Joseph Malin sought to join the British army, and fled to a group of men that he believed were British soldiers. He was wrong—they were actually American soldiers. In other words, he had attempted to join the enemy, but failed because of his own incompetence. The state of Pennsylvania indicted Malin for treason. The justices of the Pennsylvania Supreme Court, presiding over the trial, held that adhering to American troops "cannot possibly come within the idea of treason."[20] Even though Malin had a treasonous intent, his underlying conduct did not give aid and comfort to the enemy. One could imagine a variety of similar examples. Suppose someone mistakenly believes that Canada is at war with the United States and sends $1,000 to the Canadian military to aid in the "fight against the United States." Even though this person fully intended to commit treason, sending money to Canada is simply not treason.

This rough outline of the legal treatment of attempted treason was clearly valid until 1945, but it may have been significantly altered by the Supreme Court's decision in the *Cramer* case. In that case, the Supreme Court held that the prosecution must prove that the "accused *actually gave aid and comfort* to the enemy."[21] This suggests that intercepted intelligence, for example, may not constitute the basis for a treason charge, because the accused did not "actually" provide aid and comfort to the enemy. In a cryptic footnote, the Court stated, "We are not concerned here with any question as to whether there may be an offense of attempted treason."[22] On balance, the Court probably did not intend to reverse several centuries of precedent with such ambiguous language. But the Court did nothing to clarify its meaning and thus created a cloud of legal uncertainty over the issue of attempted treason. If a case of intercepted intelligence were ever prosecuted, defense counsel would likely insist that under *Cramer* no treason was committed if the intelligence did not actually reach the enemy.[23] One cannot know for sure how a court would resolve this issue, so it remains an open legal question.

Some cases of aid and comfort are quite easy to resolve; a person who joins the enemy army or who sells military equipment to the enemy has obviously committed treason. Other cases will be trickier. Buying a car for an enemy spy in the United States, for example, is an act of providing aid and comfort to the enemy if the buyer knew the recipient was a spy and did so with the intent of aiding the enemy. Similarly, giving money to a charity in the enemy's country may be treasonous if the charity can be linked to the enemy's war efforts. For example, donations to a charity to support wounded soldiers would be treason, but donations to preserve an endangered species in the enemy's country probably would not. And entering into a business transaction with a corporation located in the enemy country would be treasonous if the corporation played a role in the enemy's war efforts.[24] However, all business transactions with corporations in an enemy country are illegal under the 1917 Trading with the Enemy Act, regardless of whether the transaction has anything to do with the war.[25] In time of war, the safest move is simply to have no contact with the enemy whatsoever.

13

The Requirement of Traitorous Intent

It takes a special kind of person to be detested—and denounced as a traitor—by both Democratic United States Senator Dianne Feinstein of California and Republican United States Senator Ted Cruz of Texas, two senators who disagree about most issues of public policy. But Edward Snowden managed to create what few thought possible—a genuine moment of bipartisanship.

When Snowden's famous (or infamous) leak of mounds of American intelligence secrets to journalists became public in 2013, charges of treason echoed across the political spectrum. Senator Feinstein claimed, "I don't look at this as being a whistleblower. I think it's an act of treason." The Republican Speaker of the House John Boehner called Snowden "a traitor."[1] And in the March 3, 2016, Republican presidential primary debate, Senator Cruz, a graduate of Harvard Law School and a former law clerk to Chief Justice William Rehnquist, laid out the legal case: "The evidence is clear," Cruz asserted, "that not only [did] Snowden violate the law, but it appears he committed treason. Treason is defined under the Constitution as giving aid and comfort to the enemies of America, and what Snowden did made it easier for terrorists to avoid detection."[2]

Snowden's actions were enormously harmful to the United States and were clearly illegal under federal law. But did Snowden commit treason? For purposes of argument, we can assume that Snowden's actions made it easier for Al-Qaeda and the Taliban—who are enemies of the United States[3]—to commit acts of terror against us. Snowden, however, has insisted that he released the documents to expose illegal governmental activities and that he had no intention of aiding terrorist enemies.

The Snowden situation has parallels with other public controversies. In October 2019, Donald Trump ordered U.S. troops to abandon our Kurdish allies in Syria, an action that almost certainly helped ISIL, an enemy of the United States. Numerous ISIL fighters escaped from Kurdish custody and are now free to commit serious harm.[4] Trump has insisted, however, that he had no intention of helping ISIL, and that his actions were designed to help Turkey, a NATO ally, and to benefit the United States more generally by extricating us from decades of Middle Eastern infighting.

Or consider an earlier example from the Vietnam War. Famed American actress Jane Fonda, while on a visit to

Hanoi, the capital of North Vietnam, impulsively posed for a photograph astride an anti-aircraft gun. The photograph had significant propaganda value for the North Vietnamese, with whom the United States was at war at the time. Shortly after the visit, Fonda was denounced as a traitor by several members of Congress, and the charge has never entirely disappeared. For her part, Fonda has insisted that she posed for the picture impulsively, not quite realizing what she was doing, and had not done so with any intent to betray the United States.[5] As Fonda has recently explained, "I made a huge, huge mistake that made a lot of people think I was against the soldiers."[6] In her autobiography, Fonda claims that this photograph was her "only regret" about her trip to North Vietnam.[7]

These examples bring us to one of the most difficult issues in treason law: What is the role of intent? Is every act that might potentially aid the enemy treasonous, even if the actor had no intent to betray the country? Is it possible to commit treason inadvertently? The issue has arisen primarily in the context of aiding the enemy, so this chapter focuses on those cases, although it is relevant to levying war cases as well.

We can begin with some basic principles of criminal law.[8] To commit a crime, a person must not only commit a particular act (what lawyers call *actus reus*), she must also have the requisite mental state (what lawyers call *mens rea*). A simple example explains why. It is a crime to remove merchandise from a store without paying for it.

But suppose someone slips a candy bar from the store into your purse when you aren't looking? If you walk out of the store, you haven't committed a crime, even though you technically removed merchandise from the store without paying for it. Why not? Because you had no intent to steal.

The Model Penal Code, developed by the American Law Institute in 1962 to help standardize American criminal law, describes the four different mental states typically recognized by courts and legislatures. A person acts *purposefully* if he acts with the purpose of creating a particular result. He acts *knowingly* if he acts with the knowledge that a particular result will occur. He acts *recklessly* if he consciously disregards a substantial and unjustifiable risk that the result will occur. Finally, he acts *negligently* if he fails to adhere to the standards of conduct that a reasonable person would observe and he should have been aware that there was a substantial and unjustifiable risk that the result would occur.

To see how these mental states differ, consider some examples of gun crimes. A person acts *purposefully* if he fires a gun deliberately at another person with the intent to kill him. A person acts *knowingly* if he fires a loaded gun at another person simply because he wanted to hear the sound of gunfire. Although he didn't have a specific intent to kill, he nonetheless did something that he knew would kill or harm another person. By contrast, if a person fires a gun at another person under the mistaken apprehension that it was not loaded, we would say he acted *recklessly*, because he disregarded a substantial risk that a death would ensue. And he acts *negligently* if he accidentally leaves a loaded gun in an unlocked car, and someone then breaks into the car and uses the gun to commit a crime. Determining the relevant mental state is critical for determining the appropriate level of criminal responsibility. Purposeful crimes are punished far more severely than crimes of negligence.

The Model Penal Code was developed after the most recent treason decisions, but it is nonetheless useful for thinking about intent. The easiest case is that of a person who purposefully intends to aid the enemy. Such a person has clearly committed treason. Similarly, the decided cases make clear that merely reckless or negligent conduct cannot rise to the level of treason.[9] The hardest question is presented by a person who acts with the knowledge that his actions will aid the enemy, but without a specific purpose to do so. At least one court has found that a person who "knew, or with his knowledge had reason to know that the natural consequence of his act would be that aid and comfort would result to the enemy" had the sufficient intent to commit treason.[10] On the other hand, there is language in other cases suggesting that mere knowledge might be insufficient.[11] This point has yet to be conclusively resolved.

Under the Supreme Court's decision in the 1945 case of *Cramer v. United States*, a "defendant must not only intend the act, but he must intend to betray the country by means of the act."[12] The Court observed that there are many actions that technically provide aid and comfort to the enemy, such as "making a speech critical of the government or opposing its measures, profiteering, striking in defense plants or essential work, and the hundred other things which impair our cohesion and minimize our strength." Yet "if there is no adherence to the enemy in this, if there is no intent to betray, there is no treason."[13] That is, under *Cramer* one must both give aid and comfort to the enemy *and* do so with the intent of betraying the United States. Assuming there is legally sufficient evidence, a defendant's intent is a question of fact to be determined by a jury.

Several cases from the World War II era show this distinction at work. Hans Max Haupt, a naturalized United States citizen living in Chicago, was the father of one of the saboteurs sent to the United States by the Nazi government in 1942. When his son arrived in Chicago, Haupt provided him shelter and helped him acquire a job and an automobile. The defense argued that Haupt did so not to aid the Nazi cause, but simply out of the ordinary concern a father has for a son. The prosecution, by contrast, argued that Haupt was aware that his son was a Nazi agent and that his actions were intended to further the saboteurs' plot. The judge instructed the jury that if the father had acted only to help his son, he "must be found not guilty." But if he had intended to assist Germany or harm the United States, he was guilty. The jury convicted Haupt, and the United States Supreme Court affirmed his conviction by an 8–1 vote.[14]

In another case, three Japanese-American sisters were charged with treason for aiding two German POWs who had escaped from a Colorado POW camp.[15] The prosecution argued that the women had a traitorous intent because they knew that the men were German POWs. The defense, by contrast, argued that the women had simply acted foolishly, out of love for two men who had swayed their hearts. The jury found the women not guilty of the treason charge, but guilty on a charge of conspiracy to commit treason. The trial judge stated, "After listening to all the evidence, I did not believe the defendants had any intent to harm the United States or help the German government."[16] Accordingly, they could not be guilty of treason.

In a case from Michigan, Max Stephan was indicted for assisting Peter Krug, a German army officer who had escaped from a Canadian POW camp. Stephan was charged with providing supplies to Krug and arranging transportation for him to Chicago. The trial court charged the jury that it had to find beyond a reasonable doubt that the defendant's "intent and purpose in acting as he did was evil." If his "intent in doing what he did on the 18th and 19th days of April, 1942, was not in any way to injure this country's interest or to aid the government of Germany but merely to assist Peter Krug as an individual, the defendant must be found not guilty."[17] The jury convicted Stephan, and the conviction was upheld on appeal.[18]

Older decisions contained the same general distinction. A federal court in World War I pointed out that a person "under the domination of folly or of factional feeling or directed by a perverted view of what he is doing, or even a wrong-headed conscience" might commit acts that would otherwise be treasonous, but if the acts were done "without traitorous purpose or intent," they were not treason. "Such a man," the court stated, "plays the part of the traitor, but is not a traitor at heart."[19] Several centuries earlier, the English jurist Sir Matthew Hale noted that an officer who turned over a royal castle to the enemy was a traitor if he did so to aid the enemy or for a bribe. But if he did it because of "cowardice or imprudence without any treachery," it was not treason.[20]

It is also important to distinguish intent from motive. A defendant cannot claim, for example, that his underlying motive was to help the United States, as some defendants have claimed. A federal appellate court has explained it this way: a person who obtained American military plans during World War II and passed them to the enemy could not escape conviction for treason by arguing that "he sincerely believed his country was on the wrong side of the war" and that the country would be best served by a devastating military defeat, leading to a withdrawal from the war. It is no defense that "one acted from patriotic motives upon the sincere conviction that what he did was for the best interests of the United States."[21] Or, as the trial court in the same case explained, "Motive cannot negative an intent to betray, if you find the defendant had such an intent. Where a person has an intent to bring about a result which the law seeks to prevent, his motive is immaterial."[22] Thus, a person who sold military secrets to the enemy, for example, could not claim that his intent was only personal financial benefit. His motive might have been to make money, but he clearly intended to betray the United States in doing so.

To summarize: To be guilty of adhering to the enemy, giving them aid and comfort, a person must intend to betray the United States, either by acting with the purpose of giving aid and comfort to the enemy, or, possibly, at least with the knowledge that she is giving aid and comfort to the enemy. However, if the person acts solely because of some private consideration, such as aiding a particular individual because of a familial or romantic relationship, she lacks the requisite criminal intent. It is not a defense, however, to argue that one's underlying motives were patriotic and that one had the best interests of the United States at heart.

With these principles in mind, we can return to the cases of Edward Snowden, Donald Trump, and Jane Fonda. If Snowden had directly turned the material over to Al-Qaeda, there would be a strong case for treason. In so doing, he either intended, or had obvious reason to know, that he was giving aid and comfort to an enemy of the United States. Similarly, if Al-Qaeda had asked Snowden to leak information to a particular media outlet, the subsequent leak could be treasonous. But there doesn't appear to be any evidence that Snowden had prior contact with Al-Qaeda, nor any evidence that he intended to betray the United States or to help its enemies. By all accounts, he appears to be a naive person who honestly thought that he was doing his country a favor by leaking the information that he did. The simple reality is that government employees leak confidential material to media outlets all the time. Admittedly, most leaks are not on the scale of Snowden's, but leaking alone is not an act of treason.

Donald Trump's actions in Syria are as close as he has come to committing outright treason. Unlike his alleged conduct with respect to Russia, his actions in Syria benefited a group that is an enemy of the United States for purposes of the Treason Clause. If Trump acted with the deliberate intent to aid ISIL, his betrayal of the Kurds would amount to treason. But no publicly available evidence suggests any such intent. Trump's actions created a risk that ISIL prisoners might escape, but that was an entirely incidental consequence of his other policy goals. Under these circumstances, it would be almost impossible to establish that Trump had the necessary criminal intent of aiding the enemy.

Similarly, Jane Fonda had a strong defense to any treason charge based on her posing with a North Vietnamese anti-aircraft gun. A prosecutor would have to prove that Fonda posed for the photograph with the intent to betray the United States. Since the circumstances suggest that the photograph was almost entirely inadvertent, no reasonable prosecutor would use it as the basis for a treason charge.

Readers of a certain age will no doubt recall that the controversy over Jane Fonda in North Vietnam was about more than the photograph. Although not directly related to the issue of treasonous intent, the full scope of her activities is worth addressing here, for the simple reason that, until recent times, it has been the most high-profile dispute over the meaning of treason. Fonda's critics believe that the woman they call "Hanoi Jane" has managed to evade criminal responsibility for what they see as clear acts of treason.

During the two weeks Fonda was in North Vietnam, she engaged in six live radio broadcasts on Radio Hanoi for the North Vietnamese and recorded six more for later broadcast. All of them were specifically directed to members of the United States armed forces serving in Vietnam. Throughout the broadcasts, Fonda extensively criticized American tactics in the war, praised the people of North Vietnam, and argued that the American people did not support the war.[23] She also made statements encouraging the soldiers to stop fighting, such as the following:

> *This is Jane Fonda in Hanoi. I'm speaking to the men in the cockpits of the Phantoms, in the B-52's, in the F-4's; those of you are who still here fighting the war, in the air, on the ground; the guys in the Anglico Corps, on the 7th Fleet, the* Constellation, *the* Coral Sea, *the* Hancock, Ticonderoga, *the* Kitty Hawk, *the* Enterprise. . . . *All of you . . . know the lies . . . Knowing who was doing the lying, should you then allow these same people and same liars to define for you who your enemy is? Shouldn't we then, shouldn't we all examine the reasons that have been given to us to justify the murder that you are being paid to commit? If they told you the truth, you wouldn't fight, you wouldn't kill. You were not born and bred up by your mothers to be killers.*[24]

Although Fonda never directly encouraged soldiers to desert, as some accounts later claimed, she did urge them to put down their weapons. In this respect, Fonda's broadcasts bear similarities to those that led to the convictions in the World War II radio cases. Like those defendants, she was broadcasting on behalf of the enemy, from the enemy's capital, in time of war, and broadcasting propaganda that was potentially helpful to the enemy. Indeed, the above statement alone is more pointed than anything the government was able to prove against Iva Toguri.

Of course, everything Fonda said would be fully protected under the First Amendment if she had simply recorded these sentiments in the United States. It is also true that she honestly believed, and history bears her out on this, that the Vietnam War was a costly mistake, and that the sooner it was over, the better for everyone, including the United States. Fonda's intent was not to harm members of the American military—quite the opposite: she wanted the war over so that fewer of them would be killed. As she later put it, "I just want us *out*."[25] And there is language in some of the intent cases that suggests Fonda did not have the requisite intent to betray. But the World War II cases would have posed a substantial obstacle, as they rejected both the First Amendment and patriotic motives as defenses to a charge of broadcasting on behalf of the enemy.[26]

The Nixon administration was thus confronted with the formidable question of whether to indict Jane Fonda—one of the most famous women in the world—for treason against the United States. President Nixon, who detested Hollywood liberals and antiwar protestors, probably would have relished the thought of Jane Fonda behind bars. Although Fonda could have argued that the World War II broadcasting cases were different, it is likely that none of these arguments would have persuaded a court.

First, Fonda could have argued that the North Vietnamese were not an enemy, because there was no formal declaration of war. No American judicial decision had directly addressed that question, but, as explained in chapter 10, the English treatises and statements in other cases by American judges strongly suggested that a formal declaration of war was not necessary. Second, Fonda could have argued that she was in North Vietnam for only a few weeks, whereas the World War II defendants had all broadcast over a period of years. But Iva Toguri and Mildred Gillars had been convicted on the basis of one broadcast alone, so duration is not a necessary element of the offense. Third, Fonda could have pointed out that the World War II broadcasters were paid by the enemy, whereas she was not. But donating one's services provides even more benefit to the enemy than selling one's services. And the offense is giving aid and comfort to the enemy, not receiving it.

So why didn't the Nixon administration prosecute a case that, on the surface, at least, seemed potentially winnable? Nixon's attorney general, Richard Kleindienst, later asserted that the "damage was slight and the interest in favor of free expression was very high. . . . I thought the interests in favor of free speech in an election year far outweighed any specific advantage of prosecuting a young girl like that who was in Vietnam acting rather foolish."[27]

In this statement, Kleindienst advanced at least three separate arguments for refusing to prosecute. First, and weakest, is the condescending argument that Fonda was merely a "young girl." She was in fact thirty-four years old, older than most of the soldiers serving in Vietnam, older than Thomas Jefferson was when he drafted the Declaration of Independence, and only a few months away from constitutional eligibility to be president of the United States. Second, and somewhat stronger, is the argument that there were significant interests in free speech. Although the World War II cases rejected any free speech defense for propaganda broadcasters, the executive branch was free to interpret the First Amendment more broadly. Third, and perhaps strongest, is the lack of any real damage from Fonda's broadcasts. At the time of Fonda's visit, almost all U.S. combat troops had been removed from South Vietnam. Moreover, it seems that few of the remaining personnel even heard the broadcasts, given that the U.S. and South Vietnamese regularly jammed the Radio Hanoi signal. Perhaps most damning of all, the U.S. military itself reprinted many of her comments in the publication *Stars and Stripes* (a magazine for members of the armed forces), a tacit admission that the broadcasts were not dangerous propaganda.[28]

But Kleindienst probably wasn't being completely candid. There were at least four other reasons—some too awkward to publicly admit—to reject a prosecution of Fonda.

First, at least forty-nine Americans had made broadcasts from North Vietnam between 1965 and 1972, including prominent figures such as Stokely Carmichael, Noam Chomsky, and Eldridge Cleaver.[29] Several of these Americans had made statements far more inflammatory than anything uttered by Fonda, including a Methodist minister who urged black soldiers to join the North Vietnamese.[30] The government's consistent failure to prosecute these individuals amounted to a tacit admission that this behavior was permissible.[31] To suddenly indict Jane Fonda for what many others had done would invite serious scrutiny as to why her case was being treated differently. This concern would have been heightened significantly when, just a few weeks after Fonda's broadcasts, former U.S. attorney general Ramsey Clark (the son of former U.S. attorney general and Supreme Court Justice Tom Clark, who had initiated the treason prosecution against Iva Toguri) also broadcast from Radio Hanoi criticizing American bombing policies.[32] It would have been quite difficult to justify prosecuting Fonda without also prosecuting Clark, and the Nixon administration had no desire to indict a former attorney general of the United States.

Second, the trial would have been a media sensation, with Fonda's defense effectively putting the entire Vietnam War on trial. Just as Jefferson Davis's trial threatened to raise the issue of the legality of secession, Fonda's trial would raise, as vividly as possible, the legitimacy of the Vietnam War. Shortly after her return from North Vietnam, Fonda stated that the real "treason" was being committed by those waging "a war of aggression." The "real patriots" were "those who are doing all they can to end the war."[33] These sentiments would have reverberated through any trial.

Third, and perhaps most important, there was almost no possibility of the government obtaining a conviction. Only one juror sympathetic to the antiwar cause could force a mistrial. Federal prosecutors are notoriously risk averse and tend to bring only cases they are confident they can win. No prosecutor would have any confidence in his or her ability to convict an international superstar on a charge of treason with respect to a deeply unpopular war in the politically charged environment of the early 1970s.

Finally, it might be noted that the Nixon administration had ample reason to be hesitant about raising treason charges over Vietnam. On October 22, 1968, Nixon had ordered an aide to try to sabotage President Johnson's peace initiative. Nixon feared that peace in Vietnam would undermine his presidential campaign. When President Lyndon Johnson found out about Nixon's activities, he privately denounced them as "treason" in a phone call with Everett Dirksen, the Republican leader in the Senate.[34] A prosecution of Fonda risked exposing Nixon's own activities with respect to Vietnam, which were hardly honorable. All of these reasons suggested that even if Fonda had technically committed treason, a prosecution would have blown up in the administration's face. As a practical matter, Fonda could never have been convicted, and it would have been foolish for any prosecutor to have tried.

Treason indictments used to contain florid language about the motivation of traitors, who were typically described as "moved and seduced by the instigation of the devil." We no longer do this, but motivation remains a fundamental element of the crime. For many crimes, motivation is largely irrelevant—a person is guilty of speeding, for example, even if she didn't see the lower speed limit sign. But treason is different. It requires an intent to betray the country. As a federal appellate court put it in 1920, "Intent minus act is not treason, any more than act minus intent is."[35] There are no inadvertent traitors. And that's a good thing—no one should be convicted of the highest crime known to the law unless he or she truly and thoroughly deserves it.

14

Adam Gadahn and the War on Terror

In June 1995, Dr. Carl Pearlman, a prominent urologic surgeon, invited his sixteen-year-old grandson Adam to live with him and his wife, Agnes, at their home in Santa Ana, California. The Pearlmans were pillars of the Orange County community. Enthusiastic amateur musicians, they had helped found the Orange County Philharmonic Society and were patrons of the Idyllwild School of Music and the Arts (now the Idyllwild Arts Academy).[1] Their daughter, Nancy Pearlman, was equally successful and had established a noteworthy career as a crusading environmental journalist.[2]

The Pearlmans' only son, Philip, had chosen a different path. After a conversion to Christianity as a young adult, he had changed his name to Seth Gadahn, the surname a variant of the Biblical name Gideon. But it wasn't just his parents' ancestral Judaism that Philip/Seth rejected—it was also modernity itself. Whereas Carl Pearlman had pioneered new medical technologies, his son moved to a goat farm near the small town of Winchester in Riverside County, where he lived without electricity or running water. Adam Gadahn, along with three younger siblings, was homeschooled on the farm.[3]

The Pearlmans reasonably felt that Adam would benefit from exposure to a far broader world than he had known in Winchester. But they probably did not suspect that, of the many attractions of Orange County, he would be drawn most to the Islamic Society in Garden Grove, California. That fall, he officially converted to Islam under the guidance of Dr. Muzammil Siddiqi, a respected imam who would later meet George W. Bush in the Oval Office and lead a prayer at the National Cathedral after the September 11 attacks.[4]

We do not know how Dr. Pearlman, a secular Jew who had raised his children in a largely agnostic household, felt about his grandson's conversion to Islam. Perhaps he would have viewed it as harmless adolescent experimentation. But as a recipient of an award for promoting peace among religions, it is safe to say that he would have been appalled by the extreme version of Islam that Adam ultimately embraced.[5] Dr. Pearlman died in 1998, so he was spared the knowledge that his beloved grandson's journey to Santa Ana had concluded more horribly than he could have ever imagined. In 2015, Adam Gadahn, now a highly visible spokesman for Al-Qaeda, was killed in a CIA drone attack in Pakistan.[6] Gadahn's obituaries would note not only his extensive terrorist activities, but also the distinctive fact that he was the first American to be indicted for treason against the United States in over fifty years.

Adam Gadahn's journey, from a teenager obsessed with death metal music living on a goat farm in rural California to internationally hunted terrorist, is one of the more inexplicable stories of recent years. Yet it is a useful reminder that there is no easy way to predict who will become a traitor. It is a crime that fits no particular social profile. Although some of the men and women accused of treason in American history had obscure backgrounds, others came from positions of considerable power and privilege. With a few different choices, it's easy to imagine Adam Gadahn ending up as a doctor like his grandfather or a journalist like his aunt. Perhaps today he would still be in Southern California, quietly raising his children in a suburban cul-de-sac.

But Gadahn chose differently. A year after his conversion, he had moved out of his grandparents' house and was living with five or six other Muslim men in a small apartment near the Islamic Society. The rent was paid by Khalil Deek, a Palestinian and suspected Al-Qaeda agent, and Gadahn quickly became radicalized.[7] In 1997, Gadahn traveled to Pakistan, returning briefly a year later. It appears that from his earliest years in Pakistan, he was working with Al-Qaeda members, initially in a low-level capacity, and then gradually assuming more and more responsibility. Al-Qaeda realized the value of Gadahn's English language skills and employed him as a translator, and then, finally, as a spokesman.[8] At some point, he married an Afghan refugee, with whom he had at least one child.

In October 2004, Al-Qaeda released its first promotional video featuring Gadahn.[9] Calling himself "Azzam al-Amriki" (Azzam the American), Gadahn ranted against American intervention in the Middle East and insisted that loyalty to Allah trumped any loyalty to the country of his birth. The video ended with Gadahn's prediction that "the streets of America shall run red with blood." It was the first of many similar videos that would follow.

By now the FBI was on the case. A few months earlier, Gadahn had been named as a suspect by Attorney General John Ashcroft in a thwarted terrorist attack on Baltimore and Washington, DC.[10] Even Agnes Pearlman's house in Santa Ana was staked out by federal agents.[11] In October 2005, Gadahn was formally charged in a sealed indictment with providing material support to terrorists.

One year later, a grand jury in Santa Ana indicted Gadahn for treason, the first treason indictment in an American court since October 27, 1954.[12] The grand jury charged that Gadahn had "knowingly adhered to an enemy of the United States, namely, al-Qaeda, and gave al-Qaeda aid and comfort, within the United States and elsewhere, with intent to betray the United States." The specific charges rested on statements that Gadahn had made in five separate videos.[13] In a press release, Deputy Attorney General Paul McNulty stated, "Adam Gadahn is a U.S. citizen who made a choice to join and act as a propagandist for al Qaeda, an enemy of this country responsible for the horrific deaths of thousands of innocent Americans on Sept. 11, 2001. . . . By making this choice, we believe Gadahn committed treason—perhaps the most serious offense for which any person can be tried under our Constitution."[14] Gadahn was also added to the FBI's list of most-wanted terrorists, and the State Department offered a $1 million reward for information leading to Gadahn's capture.[15]

The Gadahn indictment bore similarities to prior treason cases, particularly those of the World War II broadcasters. Like them, Gadahn was accused of using his English-language skills to serve as a propagandist for the enemy. But Gadahn's indictment was also a legal milestone. Every previous person charged with treason for aiding the enemy had been accused of aiding a nation-state against whom the United States had formally declared war. Gadahn, by contrast, was charged with aiding a non-state actor. With this indictment, the Department of Justice had made clear that Al-Qaeda was an enemy for purposes of the Treason Clause. Presumably, if Gadahn had been captured and tried, his lawyers would have objected that aiding a terrorist group cannot amount to treason. There are no adjudicated court cases squarely resolving the issue, but a federal court in New York assumed in 2013, while addressing a different point, that an American-born Al-Qaeda member could be charged with treason against the

United States.[16] Even without such a holding, however, the Gadahn indictment is the best evidence yet that the offense of treason has not died, and that it is fully applicable in the twenty-first century.

But the Gadahn case also raises serious questions about whether such cases will ever be heard in court.

The first problem is the Constitution's requirement of two witnesses to the same overt act. In the Gadahn indictment, the government claimed to have two witnesses to each of Gadahn's broadcasts. The World War II radio broadcasting cases all assumed that a witness who merely heard the broadcasts was not a witness to the overt act. The government, at considerable expense and effort, had to bring witnesses from Tokyo, Berlin, and Rome who could testify that they personally saw the defendants making the incriminating broadcasts. In congressional hearings in 1972 over the Jane Fonda matter, a top Justice Department official testified that "there must be two perceptive witnesses to the act of broadcasting . . . in the studio where the broadcast is made. I believe that is the enunciated factor in the Axis Sally and Tokyo Rose cases."[17] Gadahn's defense lawyers would surely have insisted that the government similarly provide two witnesses who personally witnessed Gadahn recording his tapes. And it seems rather unlikely that the government had actually found two people present at the filming of the videos who would be willing and able to testify in an American court.

This requirement poses a very serious problem for prosecutors. A shrewd terrorist propagandist could easily lock himself in a room, film a propaganda video, and then e-mail the video file to websites or journalists. Under this scenario, there are no eyewitnesses to the overt act of giving aid and comfort to the enemy. Yet the evidence of treason is crystal clear. The video itself would establish beyond all doubt that the individual had aided the enemy. Indeed, it would seem to be far more reliable evidence than the testimony of two eyewitnesses. Should a traitor be allowed to escape just because he cleverly concealed his crime from witnesses?[18]

The answer may well be yes. A court could quite reasonably insist on strict adherence to the eighteenth-century Constitution, even if its provisions seem inconsistent with twenty-first-century technology. The purpose of the two-witness rule was to ensure reliability—no one would be convicted of treason without the clearest evidence of guilt. If the framers had been aware of video evidence, they might have written the Treason Clause differently. But they were not, and until the Constitution is amended, videotape evidence, standing alone, is insufficient to satisfy the two-witness requirement. This was the conclusion offered by the Justice Department in the Jane Fonda matter.[19]

On the other hand, there may be some wiggle room. Suppose FBI agents establish live video surveillance of someone they suspect may be committing treason by meeting with an enemy agent. Over the video feed, the agents observe the suspect providing military intelligence to the enemy. In this case, it would seem that there are two witnesses to the same overt act. Observing the crime through a video feed doesn't seem significantly different from, say, viewing it through a periscope while lurking behind someone's fence. If two agents testified to what they saw over the video feed, the two-witness requirement would be satisfied. We could now tweak this example slightly; instead of watching the video feed live, the agents watch a recording of the feed ten minutes later. Would testimony by those agents satisfy the two witness requirement? There is a strong pragmatic argument that it would—why should it make a critical difference whether they watched it live or watched it on a slight tape delay? If this testimony is acceptable, then it may also be acceptable to introduce evidence of people who merely watched an Al-Qaeda propaganda video and recognized the speaker.

And yet . . . there may be wisdom in the framers' two-witness requirement after all. Recent technological developments indicate that video evidence will soon become almost entirely unreliable. Using a technique known as "deep-fake," it is possible to create computer-generated videos that are almost impossible to distinguish from the real thing. Comedian Jordan Peele, for example, used this technology to create a video that appears to show Barack Obama calling Donald Trump a "total and complete dipshit."[20] Although minute examination might suggest the video is slightly off, it seems perfectly believable to a casual observer. Moreover, technological improvements will remedy the remaining glitches, and in a few years it will be almost impossible to determine whether any given video is real or fake. Video evidence of someone committing treason, far from being especially reliable, would in fact be one of the least reliable forms of evidence available. The two-witness requirement may actually function precisely as its drafters intended—as the only thing standing between an innocent person and a wrongful conviction for treason.

The second problem, of course, is that Adam Gadahn was killed by a drone and will never be tried in a United States court. This extrajudicial killing by the United States government raises very difficult questions of constitutional law. Is it permissible to simply kill a traitor with a drone, rather than going through the ordinary procedure of a criminal trial? No United States court has ever directly addressed this question.

There are strong legal arguments against drone attacks on United States citizens. These attacks, ordered by the president of the United States on the basis of intelligence assessments, are de facto executions without even the slightest hint of judicial process. The Fifth Amendment provides that no person shall be deprived of life, liberty, or property without due process of law. Even someone challenging a $25 parking ticket gets to make an argument in court. But the targets of a drone attack only learn that they have been targeted when a missile comes screaming out of the sky to kill them. The president of the United States has acted as judge, jury, and executioner. This is an extraordinary power for the president to possess. People who trusted President Obama with that power may well be less enthusiastic when it is placed in the hands of President Trump.

Nonetheless, I think drone attacks can be justified in a set of extremely narrow circumstances.[21] Due process of law doesn't always require a criminal trial. Consider an obvious example: someone begins shooting at a school with a machine gun. The police are perfectly entitled to respond by killing the shooter in order to prevent further harm. The shooter's life has been taken away by the government, but the killing was justified in the circumstances to prevent immediate harm to others. Or think about the American Civil War. President Lincoln used armed force to kill thousands of Americans who were fighting in the Confederate Army. Because they were levying war against the United States, they were appropriately subject to military force. Similarly, the United States could probably have bombed Radio Tokyo during World War II even if Iva Toguri had been present in the building.

So in some narrow circumstances the extrajudicial killing of an American citizen can be justified and is consistent with due process of law. The difficult question is determining whether drone strikes against American citizen terrorists abroad constitute one of those cases. I believe that they do, provided the following requirements are met: the target (1) is a member of a group that is a legitimate target of military action by the United States; (2) is operating in a location that is beyond the reach of ordinary law enforcement processes; and (3) is engaging in activities that pose an imminent threat to the United States. Such requirements would preclude drone strikes in most cases. It would be impermissible, for example, to use drone strikes against a Mafia leader operating in Sicily or a drug lord operating in Mexico. But in the handful of cases where we are already using military force against a foreign terrorist group, we need not hold our fire just because there is an American citizen on the other side.

The Gadahn case, charged on the basis of internet propaganda videos and concluded by a lethal drone strike, is one that could never have been contemplated by the framers of the Treason Clause, much less the drafters of the 1351 English Statute of Treasons. And yet the impulses that can lead a man from a Southern California goat farm to the target of a bull's-eye in Pakistan are as old as the ages. Treason, like it or not, is here to stay.

CONCLUSION

Over 230 years have passed since the delegates to the Constitutional Convention drafted the Treason Clause in that sweltering Assembly Room in Independence Hall. During that period, only one person, Hipolito Salazar, has been executed under federal authority for treason against the United States. Since the American Revolution, our country has felt a general unease with employing the death penalty for treason.[1] Hundreds of thousands of people levied war against the United States during the Civil War, for example, but none were executed. In the World War II era, the British hanged two men, William Joyce and John Amery, for broadcasting Nazi propaganda, yet none of their counterparts convicted in the United States received a capital sentence.[2]

Discomfort with the death penalty, however, is only part of the story. Executions for treason have been rare, but convictions have been almost equally rare, due to the Treason Clause's narrow definition of the crime. Although American treason law is in some ways broader than many people believe (its applicability to noncitizens is a striking example), it nonetheless allows a wide range of disloyal behavior to escape punishment as treason. Spying for China, even if committed by the secretary of defense, is not treason. Embezzling money from the United States Treasury and wiring it to Vladimir Putin is not treason. If levying war against the United States requires an assemblage of men, a lone individual detonating a nuclear weapon could escape indictment for treason. And the two-witness requirement means that acts of aiding the enemy committed in secret may never be punished as treason.

For many observers, these potential legal gaps suggest that our treason law might need an update. What was workable in the late 1700s is simply unsuited to the twenty-first century. A modern definition of treason would look quite different than the one handwritten in ink by men wearing long stockings and powdered wigs. We no longer dress in the eighteenth-century manner—why should we keep thinking about treason in eighteenth-century terms?

These arguments have considerable force, but I am ultimately not persuaded. The first problem is that the U.S. Constitution is almost impossible to amend. Under Article V, an amendment must pass by a two-thirds vote in both houses of Congress, and then be ratified by three-quarters of the state legislatures (alternatively, two-thirds of the states could call for a convention for proposing amendments, but this has never happened). Setting aside the anomalous Twenty-Seventh Amendment, the last time this process worked was in 1971. In a time of increased political polarization, it is hard to imagine the constitutional amendment process will generate new amendments any time soon. Expending the effort to do so is only justified if the stakes are truly significant, and modifying the definition of treason does not rise to that level.

The second reason to be wary of changes is the difficulty of determining what the new definition should contain. How broadly should the crime now sweep? There are excellent reasons for keeping the offense within fairly narrow contours. As the United States Supreme Court has explained, "the basic law of treason in this country was framed by men who . . . were taught by experience and by history to fear abuse of the treason charge almost as much as they feared treason itself."[3] And even under the narrow definition of the U.S. Constitution, the treason charge has occasionally been abused. The 1851 prosecution of Castner Hanway, a man who appears to have committed no crime whatsoever, is a perfect example. So is the case of Iva Toguri, who was prosecuted despite the Department of Justice's own professional judgment that she was innocent. A broader definition would greatly increase the possibility of abuse.

It is hard to avoid the specter of Donald Trump when thinking about this issue. Many Americans are justly appalled by Trump's behavior, and are convinced he is guilty of treason. Under this view, it is absolutely outrageous for a president to conduct himself in such a way that he appears to be a puppet of the Russian government. If such conduct is not treason under current law, then the problem is the law, which ought to be changed.

Yet the very depth of feeling against Trump is a strong

argument for caution, given that the changes we make now may last for generations. In the Aaron Burr proceedings, the Supreme Court made an eloquent plea for sobriety: "As there is no crime which can more excite and agitate the passions of men than treason, no charge demands more from the tribunal before which it is made a deliberate and temperate inquiry. Whether this inquiry be directed to the fact or to the law, none can be more solemn, none more important to the citizen or to the government; none can more affect the safety of both."[4]

In his masterful 1960 play *A Man for All Seasons*, Robert Bolt imagines a dialogue between the English lawyer Thomas More and a young man, William Roper, who is convinced that the law is not sufficiently punishing an evil person:

> **ALICE MORE:** While you talk, he's gone!
>
> **THOMAS MORE:** And go he should if he was the devil himself until he broke the law!
>
> **WILLIAM ROPER:** So now you'd give the Devil benefit of law?
>
> **THOMAS MORE:** Yes. What would you do? Cut a great road through the law to get after the Devil?
>
> **WILLIAM ROPER:** I'd cut down every law in England to do that!
>
> **THOMAS MORE:** Oh? And when the last law was down, and the Devil turned round on you—where would you hide, Roper, the laws all being flat? This country's planted thick with laws from

> coast to coast—Man's laws, not God's—and if you cut them down—and you're just the man to do it—d'you really think you could stand upright in the winds that would blow then? Yes, I'd give the Devil benefit of law, for my own safety's sake.[5]

This speech, known as the "Devil Speech," is much beloved by lawyers and law professors for its beautiful expression of the ideal of the rule of law. Bad people receive the benefit of the law, because only some type of reliable legal process can adequately distinguish good people from bad. Only a fool would permanently destroy that process just to convict one truly reprehensible person. So, too, with treason. Just as we should not cut down the law to get at the devil, neither should we broaden the definition of treason to get at Donald Trump. Because when Trump (or some future Trump) turns round on you, with the power of the federal government behind him, armed with a broader definition of treason (and, regularly tossing off frivolous accusations of treason, he's just the man to do it), what will protect you from an unwarranted prosecution? Trump's reign has produced far too many casualties already; for our own safety's sake, our nation's treason law should not be added to the fire.

The final reason for rejecting a broadening of the treason offense is the lack of any especially compelling justification to do so. No person who has committed horrific crimes against his or her country will escape punishment solely because of the language of Article III. Our espionage laws were more than capable of dealing with Julius and Ethel

Rosenberg. In proceedings arising out of the Aaron Burr case, the United States Supreme Court recognized this point, stating, "[C]rimes not clearly within the constitutional definition [of treason], should receive such punishment as the legislature in its wisdom may provide."[6] The Court reiterated this point in World War II, emphasizing that "the treason offense is not the only nor can it well serve as the principal legal weapon to vindicate our national cohesion and security. . . . Congress repeatedly has enacted prohibitions of specific acts thought to endanger our security."[7]

Indeed, I am unaware of any example in our history where a truly dangerous person escaped punishment because of the narrowness of our nation's treason laws. If such people routinely begin walking free, perhaps it is worth reconsidering the legal definition of treason. But until then, we should retain the existing legal structure that seems to work reasonably well.

And this point cannot be emphasized enough: just because something isn't treason, doesn't mean it is not a horrific crime. A serial killer is not a traitor. A producer of child pornography is not a traitor. The operator of a Ponzi scheme to defraud millions of people is not a traitor. But they are criminals nonetheless. Similarly, collaborating with a foreign government in an American election is not treason. Stuffing ballot boxes is not treason. And making improper corporate contributions to a campaign is not treason. But the people who do these things are still criminals, and our laws are fully capable of dealing with them.[8]

Disputes over treason have tended to be somewhat cyclical over American history. Periods of quiet are punctuated by periods of intense interest, such as the American Revolution, the Civil War, the aftermath of World War II, and, of course, our current heated disputes over various political figures. The contemporary rhetoric over treason will likely cool down eventually, but treason will nonetheless continue to be worthy of our attention. It is the supreme crime of American law. It has been at the center of many of our nation's most divisive controversies. And it will remain the subject of impassioned discussion for years to come, as Americans debate fundamental questions of loyalty and allegiance. That conversation will be enriched if our citizens are able to distinguish carefully between the use of "treason" as a rhetorical matter and allegations of treason as a serious criminal offense. It is my hope that this book can help all Americans to understand—and appreciate—the difference.

APPENDIX: QUIZ YOURSELF!

The following ten hypothetical questions allow you to test your basic knowledge of American treason law. (The answers appear after the questions section.)

1. A White House employee was recently quoted in the *New York Times* as stating the president was an "idiot" and "completely unprepared to lead the country in the event of a national security crisis." The president has responded by asking the Department of Justice to consider treason charges against both the employee and the *New York Times.* Have either of these parties committed treason against the United States?
2. Congress has recently enacted a law stating that it is treason for any person to divulge American national security secrets to any foreign nation or any foreign citizen. Is this law constitutional?
3. A group called Americans for Open Borders believes that all immigration laws are unjust

and unfair. They call for a nationwide attack on Customs and Border Patrol (CBP) and Immigrations and Custom Enforcement (ICE) offices on the anniversary of the 2016 presidential election. Over ten thousand people, many armed with guns, attack these offices nationwide and cause many of the offices to shut down. Federal officers manage to suppress the attacks and arrest nearly one thousand people. Can the arrestees be convicted of treason by levying war against the United States?

4. Ramona Marshall, an American citizen, recently acquired a military-grade tank. Convinced that the American government was in league with the devil, Marshall drove the tank to the Pentagon and used the tank's large gun to fire numerous rounds at the Pentagon. Marshall was finally captured, but her attack killed forty-five Pentagon employees and injured over a hundred more. Can Marshall be convicted of treason by levying war against the United States?
5. California has recently charged Gary Hanson, a California citizen, with treason against the state of California for launching a cyberattack on the state's prisons. The attack allowed numerous prisoners to escape, and the state claims that Hanson's actions constitute levying war against the state of California. Hanson has

moved to dismiss his indictment on the ground that California has no authority to prosecute cases of treason. Will Hanson's motion be granted?

6. Charles Beaumont, a French citizen, has been living in Baltimore, Maryland, for the past ten years. Recently, the federal government has learned that Beaumont has been providing significant sums of money to Al-Qaeda. Can Beaumont be convicted of treason against the United States?
7. The United States is seeking to host the 2032 Summer Olympics, as are several other nations, including Argentina. An employee of the United States Department of State, with responsibility for the U.S. Olympic bid, is secretly on the payroll of Argentina, and has provided Argentina with detailed information about the U.S. bid, including a description of the bid's strongest flaws. Recently, the employee's actions were discovered by the FBI. Can the employee be convicted of treason against the United States?
8. During World War II, a German agent secretly entered the United States. He befriended a young woman, who agreed to give him $5,000 to buy a car. The agent used the car to conduct acts of sabotage against American war industries. At the time the woman gave him the money, she did not know the man was a

German agent. Can she be convicted of treason for providing aid and comfort to the enemy?

9. During the invasion of Afghanistan following 9/11, an American citizen posted a blog entry praising the Taliban government of Afghanistan and arguing that American intervention in Afghanistan was illegal. Could he be convicted of treason for providing aid and comfort to the enemy?
10. The FBI suspects that Carla Roberts, an employee of the Department of Defense, is passing military secrets to a nation with whom the United States is at war. Late one night, an undercover agent meets with Roberts, who admits that she has transmitted military information to the enemy. Is the agent's testimony about this event sufficient to convict Roberts of treason?

ANSWERS

1. No. Under Article III of the Constitution, treason is limited to "levying war against the United States, or adhering to their enemies, giving them aid and comfort." Criticism of the president, even from a White House employee, is not an act of levying war or of adhering to enemies. The president could fire the employee, but the employee cannot be prosecuted for treason. Similarly, the *New York Times* cannot

be prosecuted for printing the employee's statement.

2. No. Under Article III, treason consists *only* of levying war against [the United States,] or adhering to their enemies, giving them aid and comfort. Congress lacks the power to alter this definition through legislation. Because some acts of espionage are not treason (for example, if the secrets are given to a nation with whom we are not at war), this statute improperly extends the constitutional definition of treason.
3. Probably not. Under late-eighteenth- and early-nineteenth-century precedents, these acts would constitute levying war against the United States. The closest analogy would be to the Whiskey Rebellion of 1794, when thousands of men marched to resist the federal excise tax on whiskey. If a court adhered to these precedents, Americans for Open Borders did commit treason. However, later cases suggest that treason by levying war requires a design to overthrow the government completely, rather than simply frustrate the operation of one particular law. Under the facts stated, there was no attempt to overthrow the government; instead, it was a riot to block the operation of a small subset of the laws. Most likely, a court will hold that such acts do not constitute treason. The rioters, however, have

still committed numerous other offenses for which they can properly be indicted.

4. Probably not. Judicial decisions have stated that levying war requires a use of force, which was present here. However, those decisions have also required that such force take the form of an "assembly of men" and have rejected the idea that a solitary individual is capable of levying war against the United States. In this case, there was no assembly of men. On the other hand, the cases interpreting levying war are quite dated, so it is possible that a court might reinterpret the levying war provision in light of modern technology to permit prosecutions of solitary individuals for the offense of levying war.
5. No. Most states recognize an offense of treason against the state, which is a distinct crime from treason against the United States. States are free to create their own definitions of treason, and states have convicted individuals of treason in the 1840s, 1850s, and 1920s. Most likely, a court would uphold a state's ability to prosecute Hanson for treason.
6. Yes. Foreign citizens resident within the United States owe a local allegiance to the United States and are subject to American treason law. Since providing aid to Al-Qaeda is a form of aiding the enemies of the United States, Beaumont can be charged with treason.

7. No. Unless the United States is in a state of open war with Argentina, providing sensitive information to Argentina is not a form of adhering to the enemy. The employee's actions are disloyal to the United States, but not all disloyalty can be prosecuted as treason.
8. No. To be convicted of treason, a person must have intended to betray the United States. Even though she gave aid and comfort to the enemy, she did not do so either purposefully or knowingly, and therefore lacked the required traitorous intent.
9. No. Criticism of American war-making, even if potentially helpful to the enemy, is protected under the First Amendment of the U.S. Constitution. Moreover, it does not appear that the writer had the required intent to betray the United States.
10. No. Under Article III, no person can be convicted of treason without the testimony of two witnesses to the same overt act, or confession in open court. The agent did not directly observe an overt act of treason, and even if he had, two witnesses would be required. Roberts's confession is not sufficient for conviction since it was not made in open court.

ACKNOWLEDGMENTS

I would never have written this book without the encouragement of my literary agent, Wendy Strothman, who has believed in this project from the beginning. I am deeply grateful for all of her efforts. Lauren MacLeod conducted the auction and cheerfully helped with numerous details.

Special thanks to Dean Kevin Johnson and Associate Dean Afra Afsharipour at the UC Davis School of Law for their support and for summer research funding. The librarians at the Mabie Law Library performed heroic labors in tracking down sources. The Committee on Research of the UC Davis Academic Senate provided financial support.

Some of the ideas in this book were initially developed in op-eds for the *Washington Post* and for the *Take Care Blog*. I am grateful to Adam Kushner at the *Post* and Joshua Matz at *Take Care* for the opportunities. The feedback I received from readers, including Graham Dodge, Irving Greines, and Robert Hugins, was helpful in thinking through these issues. Ashutosh Bhagwat and Brian

Soucek helped clarify my thoughts on the First Amendment.

At Ecco, Denise Oswald has been a superb editor, with a keen eye for clarity and concision. Norma Barksdale kept everything running smoothly.

My parents, Carl and Esther Larson, read the entire manuscript twice and provided numerous helpful suggestions.

Finally, my deepest thanks are owed to my family. My wife, Elaine Lau, carefully read the manuscript, and her editorial insights have improved it significantly. My children, Carina and Elliot, make every day better. This book is for them.

NOTES

INTRODUCTION

1. Zachary Basu, "The 24 Times Trump Accused Someone of 'Treason,'" Axios, June 16, 2019, https://www.axios.com/trump-treason-russia-investigation-new-york-times-e1660029-c73c-4809-8bd5-8988f1ed4fda.html.
2. "Trump Accuses FBI Agent Removed from Mueller Probe of Committing 'Treason,'" Politico, January 12, 2018, https://www.politico.com/story/2018/01/12/trump-peter-strzok-treason-337918.
3. Jessica Taylor, "Trump: Democrats 'Un-American,' 'Treasonous' during State of the Union," NPR, February 5, 2018, https://www.npr.org/2018/02/05/583447413/trump-democrats-un-american-treasonous-during-state-of-the-union.
4. Conor Friedersdorf, "A President Falsely Charging 'Treason' Is What the Founders Feared," *Atlantic*, April 11, 2019, https://www.theatlantic.com/ideas/archive/2019/04/trump-treason/586915/.
5. Philip Bump, "Trump, Not Understanding Treason, Names People He Thinks Committed the Capital Crime," *Washington Post*, May 23, 2019.

6. Basu, "24 Times"; Daniel Dale, "Fact Check: Trump Made Seven False Claims to Sean Hannity," CNN, July 26, 2019, https://www.cnn.com/2019/07/26/politics/fact-check-trump-hannity-july-phone-interview/index.html.
7. Katie Rogers, "As Impeachment Talk Moves Forward, Trump's Language Turns Darker," *New York Times*, October 2, 2019, A13.
8. "BREAKING: Chuck Schumer Just Got The WORST NEWS EVER!—Treason Charges Probable," *ENH Live* (defunct), March 2017, http://hillaryclinton.trendolizer.com/2017/03/breaking-chuck-schumer-just-got-the-worst-news-ever-treason-charges-probable.html.
9. A. M. Smith, "BREAKING: Trump U.S. District Attorney to Pursue TREASON Charges Against Barack Obama!," en Volve, February 21, 2017, http://en-volve.com/2017/02/21/breaking-trump-u-s-district-attorney-to-pursue-treason-charges-against-barack-obama/.
10. James H. Chesky, "Try U.S,. [*sic*] Senator Mitch McConnell for Treason," petition, MoveOn.org, http://petitions.moveon.org/sign/try-us-senator-mitch.
11. ALLIGATOR! in Los Angeles, "Indict DNC Chair Debbie Wassermann [*sic*] Schultz and DNC Co-conspirators for TREASON!," petition, Change.org, https://www.change.org/p/fbi-director-james-comey-indict-debbie-wasserman-schultz-for-treason.
12. Julia Brucculieri, "Jon Voight Thinks Miley Cyrus and Shia LaBeouf Are 'Teaching Treason,'" Huffington Post, January 25, 2017.
13. "Colin Kaepernick Branded a 'Traitor' by NFL Executives Over Anthem Protest," *Guardian*, August 31, 2016.
14. The execution procedure is described in William Black-

stone, *Commentaries on the Laws of England* (Oxford, UK: Clarendon Press, 1769), 4:92.

15. *Cramer v. United States*, 325 U.S. 1, 46–47 (1945).
16. In 1892, a law journal noted, "The learning on the doctrine of high treason, although voluminous, is more familiar to the antiquary than to the practitioner." Roger Foster, "Treason Trials in the United States," *Albany Law Journal* 46 (1892): 345–47.
17. The Treason Clause of Article III means that American treason law is a subset of American constitutional law, a field notoriously plagued by controversy over methodological issues. At the very broadest level there are disputes between those who believe that constitutional meaning is relatively fixed at the time of enactment and those who favor more of a "living constitution" approach. There are also disputes over how much weight to give to strictly textual arguments, to prior judicial decisions, and to pragmatic considerations.

    This book does not attempt to resolve any of these disputes or to advance any particular methodological agenda. Suffice it to say that American courts, including the Supreme Court, apply a wide variety of methodologies when deciding cases. My goal is to provide the fairest reading I can of the law, using the decided cases and whatever other materials might be relevant. In thinking about how courts might address unresolved issues, I try to consider the various methodologies and arguments that might be employed on either side.

    One point, however, bears mentioning. In some places the Constitution uses terms that are clearly drawn from English law and that have a very distinct meaning under

English law. Such terms include "writ of habeas corpus" and "letters of marque and reprisal." These terms have a very limited range of interpretation (for example, a writ of habeas corpus cannot be interpreted as a writ of replevin). In other places, the Constitution employs capacious language that almost seems to invite judicial interpretation in accordance with the felt needs of the times. Such phrases include "due process of law" and "equal protection of the laws."

The terms "levying war against the United States" and "adhering to their enemies, giving them aid and comfort" are much closer to "writ of habeas corpus" than they are to "due process of law." They had a distinctive meaning under English law, and American courts have consistently relied on English law to interpret them. As explained in chapter 1, it is possible that modern American treason law is narrower than eighteenth-century English treason law, but it is not plausible that it is broader.

1: THE ENGLISH ORIGINS OF AMERICAN TREASON LAW AND THE ADOPTION OF THE CONSTITUTION'S TREASON CLAUSE

The leading work on American treason law is James Willard Hurst, *The Law of Treason in the United States* (Westport, CT: Greenwood, 1971). For treason law during the American Revolution, see Carlton F. W. Larson, *The Trials of Allegiance: Treason, Juries, and the American Revolution* (New York: Oxford University Press, 2019). On treason law in medieval England, see J. G. Bellamy, *The Law of Treason in England in the Later Middle Ages* (Cambridge: Cambridge University Press, 1970).

1. The date for this statute is sometimes given as 1352. The discrepancy arises from the date of the New Year, which

in the 1300s was March 25. The Statute of Treasons was enacted in January 1351, according to the older dating. Modern dating would treat the month as January 1352.

2. J. G. Bellamy, *The Law of Treason in England in the Later Middle Ages* (Cambridge: Cambridge University Press, 1970), 100.
3. For an overview, see J. H. Baker, *An Introduction to English Legal History*, 4th ed. (London: Reed Elsevier, 2002), 223–45.
4. Bellamy, *Law of Treason*, 71, 79–82.
5. Edward Coke, *The Third Part of the Institutes of the Laws of England*, 5th ed. (1671), 2.
6. James Wilson, "Lectures on Law," in *The Works of James Wilson*, ed. Robert Green McCloskey (Cambridge, MA: Harvard University Press, 1967), 2:664–65.
7. *United States v. Burr*, 25 F. Cas. 1, 13 (C.C.D. Va. 1807) (No. 14,692) (Marshall, C.J.).
8. *United States v. Hoxie*, 26 F. Cas. 397, 398 (C.C.D. Vt. 1808) (No. 15,407) (Livingston, J.).
9. See, e.g., Francia's Case (1717), *Reports of Sir Peter King, Chief Justice of Common Pleas, 1714–1722*, eds. Lloyd Bonfield & L.R. Poos (London: Selden Society, 2017), 82–84.
10. In *Haupt v. United States*, 330 U.S. 631, 642–643 (1947), the United States Supreme Court held that out-of-court confessions were admissible in treason cases, so long as they were merely corroborative of testimony already established by two witnesses to the same overt act.
11. Carlton F. W. Larson, *The Trials of Allegiance: Treason, Juries, and the American Revolution* (New York: Oxford University Press, 2019), 271 n.33.
12. 18 U.S.C. § 2381.

13. For a broad discussion of this issue, see James Willard Hurst, *The Law of Treason in the United States: Collected Essays* (Westport, CT: Greenwood Publishing, 1971), 145–66.
14. *Ex parte Bollman*, 8 U.S. 75, 127 (1807).
15. *United States v. Wimmer*, 264 F. 11, 13 (6th Cir. 1920); see also *United States v. Rosenberg*, 195 F.2d 583, 611 (2d Cir. 1952).
16. Hurst, *Law of Treason*, 149.

2: BENEDICT ARNOLD: FOUNDING TRAITOR

The classic work on Arnold's treason is Carl Van Doren, *The Secret History of the American Revolution* (New York: Viking Press, 1941). The best recent account is Stephen Brumwell, *Turncoat* (New Haven: Yale University Press, 2018). The story is vividly related in Nathaniel Philbrick, *Valiant Ambition: George Washington, Benedict Arnold, and the Fate of the American Revolution* (New York: Penguin, 2016). For a biography through the Battle of Saratoga, see James Kirby Martin, *Benedict Arnold, Revolutionary Hero: An American Warrior Reconsidered* (New York: NYU Press, 1997). For a full biography, see Willard Sterne Randall, *Benedict Arnold: Patriot and Traitor* (New York: William Morrow, 1990).

1. Alexander Hamilton to Elizabeth Schuyler, September 25, 1780, in *The Papers of Alexander Hamilton*, ed. Harold C. Syrett (New York: Columbia University Press, 1961), 2:441–42.
2. To be sure, the question of Peggy Arnold's guilt continues to be debated. The modern scholarly consensus, however, strongly supports the conclusion that she was well aware of what her husband was up to. Stephen Brumwell, *Turncoat: Benedict Arnold and the Crisis of American Liberty*

(New Haven: Yale University Press, 2018), 168–69; Nancy Rubin Stuart, *Defiant Brides: The Untold Story of Two Revolutionary Era Women and the Radical Men They Married* (Boston: Beacon Press, 2013), 70, 79, 95–100, 135; Mark Jacob and Stephen H. Case, *Treacherous Beauty: Peggy Shippen, the Woman behind Benedict Arnold's Plot to Betray America* (Guilford, CT: Lyons Press, 2012), viii, 1, 164–65, 170. For a dissenting view, see Joyce Lee Malcolm, *The Tragedy of Benedict Arnold: An American Life* (New York: Pegasus Books, 2018), 288–89, 326–27.

3. Quoted in Brumwell, *Turncoat*, 280.
4. See "England & Wales Baby Names," http://names.darkgreener.com/#benedict.
5. This information can be found at the Social Security website, https://www.ssa.gov/oact/babynames/.
6. Brumwell, *Turncoat*, 74; James Kirby Martin, *Benedict Arnold, Revolutionary Hero: An American Warrior Reconsidered* (New York: NYU Press, 1997), 409.
7. Brumwell, *Turncoat*, 159–69.
8. Willard Sterne Randall, *Benedict Arnold: Patriot and Traitor* (New York: William Morrow, 1990), 522–24.
9. Nathaniel Philbrick, *Valiant Ambition: George Washington, Benedict Arnold, and the Fate of the American Revolution* (New York: Penguin, 2016), 300–302.
10. "General Orders, 26 September 1780," Founders Online, National Archives, last modified June 13, 2018, http://founders.archives.gov/documents/Washington/99-01-02-03388.
11. Larson, *Trials of Allegiance*, 96–100, 199.
12. William Emery Decrow, *Yale and the "City of Elms"* (Boston: W. E. Decrow, 1882), 117.

13. Martin, *Benedict Arnold*, 430.
14. Larson, *Trials of Allegiance*, 199.
15. Quoted in Stuart, *Defiant Brides*, 135.
16. Larson, *Trials of Allegiance*, 223–26.
17. Randall, *Benedict Arnold*, 602.
18. Robert A. Ferguson, *Reading the Early Republic* (Cambridge, MA: Harvard University Press, 2004), 122.
19. Quoted in Brumwell, *Turncoat*, 300.
20. Randall, *Benedict Arnold*, 599; Stuart, *Defiant Brides*, 201.
21. Randall, *Benedict Arnold*, 615.
22. Saratoga Monument Virtual Tour part 3, National Parks Service, https://www.nps.gov/sara/learn/photosmultimedia/saratoga-monument-virtual-tour-part-3.htm.
23. Saratoga Monument Virtual Tour part 6, National Parks Service, https://www.nps.gov/sara/learn/photosmultimedia/saratoga_monument_virtual_tour_part_6.htm.
24. Martin, *Benedict Arnold*, 432.
25. Quoted in Brumwell, *Turncoat*, 315.
26. Erik Ofgang, "Burning Benedict Arnold's Effigy in New London, *Connecticut Magazine*, September 6, 2017, http://www.connecticutmag.com/the-connecticut-story/burning-benedict-arnold-s-effigy-in-new-london/article_266ec4bc-82c4-11e7-9495-a3826d6158b3.html.

3: WHAT IS "LEVYING WAR AGAINST THE UNITED STATES"?

The leading work on American treason law is James Willard Hurst, *The Law of Treason in the United States: Collected Essays* (Westport, CT: Greenwood Publishing, 1971). For a more recent analysis in the terrorism context, see Carlton F. W. Larson, "The Constitutional Law of Treason and the Enemy Combatant Problem," *University of Pennsylvania Law Review* 154 (2006):

863–926. On the levying war arguments in the Whiskey Rebellion and Fries's Rebellion cases, see Carlton F. W. Larson, *The Trials of Allegiance: Treason, Juries, and the American Revolution* (New York: Oxford University Press, 2019), chapter 9.

1. Michael Foster, *A Report of Some Proceedings on the Commission of Oyer and Terminer and Goal Delivery for the Trial of the Rebels in the Year 1746 in the County of Surry; and of Other Crown Cases: To Which Are Added Discourses upon a Few Branches of the Crown Law* (Oxford: Clarendon Press, 1762), 210–11.
2. Ibid., 211.
3. *United States v. Burr*, 25 F. Cas. 55, 159 (C.C. Va. 1807) (No. 14,693). Marshall echoed the point a few pages later: "[T]he term, having been adopted by our constitution, must be understood in that sense in which it was universally received in this country when the constitution was framed. The sense in which it was received is to be collected from the most approved authorities of that nation from which we have borrowed the term." Ibid., 163.
4. Thomas McKean, Notes of Charges Delivered to Grand Juries by Chief Justice Thomas McKean, 1777–1779, 25–27, Historical Society of Pennsylvania, Philadelphia.
5. Wilson, "Lectures on Law," 2:668.
6. *United States v. Burr*, 25 F. Cas. 55, 161 (C.C.D. Va. 1807) (No. 14,693) (Marshall, C. J.).
7. On the Whiskey Rebellion, see generally Thomas P. Slaughter, *The Whiskey Rebellion: Frontier Epilogue to the American Revolution* (New York: Oxford University Press, 1988).
8. United States v. Mitchell, 2 U.S. (2 Dall.) 348, 355 (C.C.D. Pa. 1795).

9. Case of Fries, 9 F. Cas. 924, 943-944 (C.C.D. Pa. 1800) (No. 5127).
10. John Adams to James Lloyd, March 31, 1815, *Works of John Adams* (Boston: Little, Brown & Co., 1856), 10:152–55.
11. Burr, 25 F. Cas. at 168–69.
12. Charge to the Grand Jury—Treason, 30 F. Cas. 1046, 1047 (C.C.D.R.I. 1842) (No. 18,275) (Story, J.).
13. *United States v. Hoxie*, 26 F. Cas. 397, 398 (C.C.D. Vt. 1808) (No. 15,407) (Livingston, J.).
14. *United States v. Hanway*, 26 F. Cas. 105, 127–28 (C.C.E.D. Pa. 1851) (No. 15,299) (Grier, J.).
15. Quoted in "Indictments Stand at Miners' Trial," *New York Times*, April 26, 1922, 18.
16. Bradley Chapin, *The American Law of Treason: Revolutionary and Early National Origins* (Seattle: University of Washington Press), 97.
17. Hurst, *Law of Treason*, ix.
18. Ibid., 7; see also ibid., 270–73.
19. *United States v. Burr*, 25 F. Cas. 2, 13 (C.C.D. Va. 1807) (No. 14,692a).
20. *United States v. Burr*, 25 F. Cas., 55, 165 (C.C.D. Va. 1807) (No. 14,693) (emphasis added).
21. Ibid., 169.
22. Charge to the Grand Jury—Treason, 30 F. Cas. 1046, 1047 (C.C.D.R.I. 1842) (No. 18,275) (Story, J.).

4: THE CASE OF AARON BURR

The most accessible introduction to Burr is David O. Stewart, *American Emperor: Aaron Burr's Challenge to Jefferson's America* (New York: Simon & Schuster, 2011). For a full biography of Burr, see Nancy Isenberg, *Fallen Founder: The Life of Aaron*

Burr (New York: Penguin, 2007). Two recent books focus on Burr's treason trial: Peter Charles Hoffer, *The Treason Trials of Aaron Burr* (Lawrence, KS: University Press of Kansas, 2008); and R. Kent Newmyer, *The Treason Trial of Aaron Burr: Law, Politics, and the Character Wars of the New Nation* (Cambridge: Cambridge University Press, 2012). For an overview of public reaction to Burr, see James E. Lewis Jr., *The Burr Conspiracy: Uncovering the Story of an Early American Crisis* (Princeton, NJ: Princeton University Press, 2017). The Burr trial is reported at *United States v. Burr*, 25 F. Cas. 1 (C.C. Va. 1807) (No. 14,692); and *United States v. Burr*, 25 F. Cas. 55 (C.C. Va. 1807) (No. 14,693).

1. James E. Lewis Jr., *The Burr Conspiracy: Uncovering the Story of an Early American Crisis* (Princeton, NJ: Princeton University Press, 2017), 166.
2. Ibid., 339–68.
3. See Andro Linklater, *An Artist in Treason: The Extraordinary Double Life of General James Wilkinson* (New York: Walker, 2009).
4. Quoted in David O. Stewart, *American Emperor: Aaron Burr's Challenge to Jefferson's America* (New York: Simon & Schuster, 2011), 208.
5. Ibid., 19.
6. The indictment can be read in ibid., 313–15.
7. *Ex parte Bollman*, 8 U.S. (4 Cranch) 75, 127 (1807).
8. Ibid., 126.
9. Ibid., 126.
10. *United States v. Burr*, 25 F. Cas. 2, 15 (C.C. Va. 1807) (No. 14,692a).
11. Stewart, *American Emperor*, 233; Lewis, *Burr Conspiracy*, 425–26.

12. Stewart, *American Emperor*, 231.
13. Peter Charles Hoffer, *The Treason Trials of Aaron Burr* (Lawrence, KS: University Press of Kansas, 2008), 159.
14. *Burr*, 25 F. Cas. at 177.
15. Ibid., 180.
16. Stewart, *American Emperor*, 242, 260. Following his acquittal for treason, he was prosecuted and acquitted on a misdemeanor charge of violating the Neutrality Act before Chief Justice Marshall in Richmond, and then ordered to stand trial in Ohio on a similar charge. The Jefferson administration, however, later dropped the Ohio charge. R. Kent Newmyer, *The Treason Trial of Aaron Burr: Law, Politics, and the Character Wars of the New Nation* (Cambridge: Cambridge University Press, 2012), 168–70.
17. Quoted in Hoffer, *Treason Trials of Aaron Burr*, 172.
18. Lewis, *Burr Conspiracy*, 394.
19. Hannah Natanson, "Aaron Burr—Villain of 'Hamilton'—Had a Secret Family of Color, New Research Shows," *Washington Post*, August 24, 2019.
20. Lewis, *Burr Conspiracy*, 114.
21. Stewart, *American Emperor*, 300–301.
22. Hoffer, *Treason Trials of Aaron Burr*, 189–93.

5: THE FORGOTTEN CRIME OF TREASON AGAINST A STATE

The most significant studies of the Dorr Rebellion are Marvin E. Gettleman, *The Dorr Rebellion: A Study in American Radicalism* (New York: Random House, 1973; reprint, New York: Robert E. Krieger, 1980); and George M. Dennison, *The Dorr War: Republicanism on Trial, 1831–1861* (Lexington, KY: University Press of Kentucky, 1976). The first major academic study was Arthur May Mowry, *The Dorr War, or the Constitutional*

Struggle in Rhode Island (Providence, RI: Preston & Rounds, 1901). For a brisk narrative with illustrations of locations related to the Rebellion, see Rory Raven, *The Dorr War: Treason, Rebellion & the Fight for Reform in Rhode Island* (Charleston, SC: History Press, 2010). Dorr's trial is reported in "The Trial of Thomas Wilson Dorr for Treason, Rhode Island, 1844," *American State Trials*, ed. John D. Lawson (St. Louis: F.H. Thomas Law Book Co., 1914), 2:5–170; and Joseph S. Pitman, *Report of the Trial of Thomas Wilson Dorr for Treason* (Boston: Tappan & Denner, 1844).

The best book on John Brown's trial is Brian McGinty, *John Brown's Trial* (Cambridge, MA: Harvard University Press, 2009). The trial, along with those of Brown's associates, is reported in *American State Trials*, ed. John D. Lawson (St. Louis: F.H. Thomas Law Book Co., 1916), 6:700–864. For an engaging account of the raid, see Tony Horwitz, *Midnight Rising: John Brown and the Raid That Sparked the Civil War* (New York: Henry Holt, 2011). For a thorough biography of Brown, see Stephen B. Oates, *To Purge This Land With Blood: A Biography of John Brown*, 2nd ed. (Amherst, MA: University of Massachusetts Press, 1984).

The leading modern work on the Mine Wars is James Green, *The Devil Is Here in These Hills: West Virginia's Coal Miners and Their Battle for Freedom* (New York: Atlantic Monthly Press, 2015). Also useful is Lon Savage, *Thunder in the Mountains: The West Virginia Mine War, 1920–1921* (Pittsburgh: University of Pittsburgh Press, 2014); and Howard B. Lee, *Bloodletting in Appalachia: The Story of West Virginia's Four Major Mine Wars and Other Thrilling Incidents of Its Coal Fields* (Morgantown, WV: West Virginia University, 1969). For selected primary sources, see David Alan Corbin, ed., *Gun Thugs, Rednecks, and Radicals:*

A Documentary History of the West Virginia Mine Wars (Oakland, CA: PM Press, 2011). The Mine Wars are the subject of a well-done PBS American Experience documentary *The Mine Wars*, as well as the 1987 Hollywood production *Matewan*.

The most thorough modern legal analysis of treason against a state is J. Taylor McConkie, "State Treason: The History and Validity of Treason Against Individual States," *Kentucky Law Journal* 101 (2012–2013): 281–336.

1. The seven that do not are Hawaii, Maryland, New Hampshire, New York, Ohio, Pennsylvania, and Tennessee. Twenty-one other states define the offense in their state constitutions only. Because these states have not enacted a separate criminal statute regarding treason, it is likely that treason against the state is not technically a crime in these states. J. Taylor McConkie, "State Treason: The History and Validity of Treason Against Individual States," *Kentucky Law Journal* 101 (2012–2013): 297, 299.
2. Or. Rev. Stat. § 166.005.
3. See generally Larson, *Trials of Allegiance*.
4. Ibid., 65
5. McConkie, "State Treason," 334.
6. The text of the People's Constitution can be found in Marvin E. Gettleman, *The Dorr Rebellion: A Study in American Radicalism* (New York: Random House, 1973; reprint, New York: Robert E. Krieger, 1980), 205–31.
7. Ibid., 54.
8. The text of the act can be found at *Newport Mercury*, April 9, 1842, 2.
9. Gettleman, *Dorr Rebellion*, 12–15.
10. Quoted in ibid., 86.
11. Gettleman, *Dorr Rebellion*, 160–61, n. 79. Several other

men may also have been tried. George M. Dennison, *The Dorr War: Republicanism on Trial, 1831–1861* (Lexington, KY: University Press of Kentucky, 1976), 146.

12. "The Trial of Thomas Wilson Dorr for Treason, Rhode Island, 1844," *American State Trials*, ed. John D. Lawson (St. Louis: F.H. Thomas Law Book Co., 1914), 2:50.
13. Ibid., 2:164 n.20.
14. *Luther v. Borden*, 48 U.S. 1 (1849).
15. Tony Horwitz, *Midnight Rising: John Brown and the Raid That Sparked the Civil War* (New York: Henry Holt, 2011), 291–92.
16. On this document, see Robert L. Tsai, *America's Forgotten Constitutions* (Cambridge, MA: Harvard University Press, 2014), 83–117.
17. Brian McGinty, *John Brown's Trial* (Cambridge, MA: Harvard University Press, 2009), 6–7.
18. Louis DeCaro Jr., *Freedom's Dawn: The Last Days of John Brown in Virginia* (Lanham, MD: Rowman & Littlefield, 2015), 87.
19. McGinty, *John Brown's Trial*, 271. Treason charges against a third raider, John Cook, were dropped by the prosecution. On Cook, see Steven Lubet, *John Brown's Spy: The Adventurous Life and Tragic Confession of John E. Cook* (New Haven: Yale University Press, 2012).
20. Quoted in Horwitz, *Midnight Rising*, 254.
21. Quoted in McGinty, *John Brown's Trial*, 260.
22. Ibid., 111, 242.
23. Horwitz, *Midnight Rising*, 256.
24. James Green, *The Devil Is Here in These Hills: West Virginia's Coal Miners and Their Battle for Freedom* (New York: Atlantic Monthly Press, 2015), 262, 264.
25. Lon Savage, *Thunder in the Mountains: The West Virginia*

Mine War, 1920–1921 (Pittsburgh: University of Pittsburgh Press, 2014), 161.

26. "'Treason' in West Virginia," *New York Times*, May 30, 1922, 9.
27. Green, *Devil Is Here*, 299–302; Howard B. Lee, *Bloodletting in Appalachia: The Story of West Virginia's Four Major Mine Wars and Other Thrilling Incidents of Its Coal Fields* (Morgantown, WV: West Virginia University, 1969), 111. Allen's conviction was so obscure that the nation's most eminent treason scholar, James Willard Hurst, was entirely unaware of it just a few decades later. Hurst, *Law of Treason*, 187 (stating that Dorr and Brown were the "only completed treason prosecutions by state authorities").
28. Lee, *Bloodletting in Appalachia*, 114.
29. Although Dorr, Brown, Coppoc, and Allen remain the only individuals convicted of treason against a state since the U.S. Constitution was adopted, there were a handful of other attempted prosecutions that did not result in conviction. An indictment of three men for treason against New York during the War of 1812 was rejected by a New York court on the ground that the offense amounted to treason against the United States. *People v. Lynch*, 11 Johns 549 (N.Y. Sup. Ct. 1814). In the 1830s and 1840s, indictments were brought against Mormon leaders for treason against Missouri and treason against Illinois, but none of the cases went to trial. Hurst, *Law of Treason*, 264; McConkie, "State Treason," 310–12. And in 1892, thirty-one labor agitators were indicted for treason against Pennsylvania for their actions during the Homestead Strike. *Commonwealth v. O'Donnell*, et al., 12 Pa. Co. 97 (Pa. O.&T. 1892). Legal experts mocked the Pennsylvania in-

dictments, claiming they were a "mass of stale, medieval verbiage." How a labor strike, even a violent one, could "be dignified into the crime of treason, passes professional comprehension." "Treason Trials in the United States," *American Law Review* 26 (1892): 912–14. Pennsylvania officials quietly let the treason charges drop, while pursuing prosecutions on other counts.

30. Max Farrand, *The Records of the Federal Convention of 1787*, rev. ed. (New Haven: Yale University Press, 1966), 347–49.
31. "Trial of Thomas Wilson Dorr," *American State Trials*, 2:154; James G. Randall, "The Miners and the Law of Treason," *The North American Review* 216 (1922): 312, 321–22.
32. Quoted in Randall, "Miners and the Law of Treason," 321–22.
33. Joseph Story, Charge to Grand Jury—Treason, 30 F. Cas. 1046 (C.C.D.R.I. 1842).
34. *People v. Lynch*, 11 Johns 549, 553 (N.Y. Sup. Ct. 1814).
35. "Francis Dana's Charge, Cumberland, Essex, Hampshire, Lincoln, Plymouth, & York Counties, May–July 1792," in *Gentlemen of the Grand Jury: The Surviving Grand Jury Charges from Colonial, State, and Lower Federal Courts before 1801*, ed. Stanton D. Krauss (Durham, NC: Carolina Academic Press, 2012), 1:409, 410.
36. An 1805 South Carolina statute, for example, included inciting slave rebellions as a form of treason against the state. McConkie, "State Treason," 294. In an 1850 message, President Millard Fillmore stated, "Texas is a State, authorized . . . to punish those who may commit treason against the State according to the forms provided by her own constitution and her own laws." Millard Fillmore to

Senate and House of Representatives, August 6, 1850, *A Compilation of the Messages and Papers of the Presidents*, ed. James D. Richardson (New York: Bureau of National Literature, 1897), 6:2605.

37. See, e.g., *Kennedy v. Louisiana*, 554 U.S. 407 (2008).

6: THE CASE OF CASTNER HANWAY AND THE FUGITIVE SLAVE ACT

The leading work on the Christiana Riot is Thomas P. Slaughter, *Bloody Dawn: The Christiana Riot and Racial Violence in the Antebellum North* (New York: Oxford University Press, 1991). The Hanway trial and the Fugitive Slave Act are examined extensively in Steven Lubet, *Fugitive Justice: Runaways, Rescuers, and Slavery on Trial* (Cambridge, MA: Harvard University Press, 2010). W. U. Hensel, *The Christiana Riot and the Treason Trials of 1851* (Lancaster, PA: New Era Printing Co., 1911), although dated, nonetheless contains useful information, especially on the jury pool. It also reprints William Parker's narrative of the events. Jonathan Katz, *The Resistance at Christiana: The Fugitive Slave Rebellion, Christiana, Pennsylvania, September 11, 1851, A Documentary Account* (New York: Thomas Y. Crowell, 1974), contains excerpts from numerous primary documents as well as useful photographs. The official report of the Hanway trial is published as *United States v. Hanway*, 26 F. Cas. 105 (C.C.E.D. Pa. 1851) (No. 15,299). My factual account of the underlying events and the trial is drawn from these sources. On the history of Independence Hall, see Charlene Mires, *Independence Hall in American Memory* (Philadelphia: University of Pennsylvania Press, 2002).

1. On these trials, see Larson, *Trials of Allegiance*.
2. *Daily National Intelligencer*, November 25, 1851.
3. Larson, *Trials of Allegiance*, 236.

4. Act of Sept. 16, 1850, chap. 60, *Statutes at Large*, 9:462.
5. Charlene Mires, *Independence Hall in American Memory* (Philadelphia: University of Pennsylvania Press, 2002), 94.
6. Michael W. Kauffman, *American Brutus: John Wilkes Booth and the Lincoln Conspiracies* (New York: Random House, 2004), 88.
7. I constructed the family relationship from genealogical material available on Ancestry.com.
8. Thomas P. Slaughter, *Bloody Dawn: The Christiana Riot and Racial Violence in the Antebellum North* (New York: Oxford University Press, 1991), 56–57.
9. "The Murder of Southern Men," *Georgia Telegraph*, September 30, 1851, 2.
10. "Mass Meeting in Baltimore," *Daily Morning News*, September 20, 1851.
11. Slaughter, *Bloody Dawn*, 106–107, 116–17.
12. Michael P. Dougan, "Grier, Robert Cooper," in *The Oxford Companion to the Supreme Court of the United States*, ed. Kermit L. Hall (New York: Oxford University Press, 1992), 349–50.
13. *Hanway*, 26 F. Cas., at 109.
14. W. U. Hensel, *The Christiana Riot and the Treason Trials of 1851* (Lancaster, PA: New Era Printing Co., 1911), 73.
15. Slaughter, *Bloody Dawn*, 117–18, 122–23.
16. *Hanway*, 26 F. Cas., at 110–12.
17. "The Fugitive Law Illustrated," *Frederick Douglass' Paper*, October 2, 1851.
18. "Pennsylvania Treason Trials," *Georgia Telegraph*, December 16, 1851, 2.
19. "Indictment for Treason," *Baltimore Sun*, September 26, 1851, reprinted in *Daily Morning News*, September 30, 1851.
20. *Hanway*, 26 F. Cas., at 116.

21. Ibid., 117–21.
22. Ibid., 121–23.
23. Ibid., 127–28.
24. "The Treason Trials-Correspondence of the New York Herald," *Cleveland Herald*, December 22, 1851.
25. "The Christiana Trials—From the Baltimore Clipper," *Daily National Intelligencer*, February 5, 1852.

7: WHO IS SUBJECT TO AMERICAN TREASON LAW?

1. *New York Times Co. v U.S. Dep't of Justice*, 915 F.Supp.2d 508 (S.D.N.Y. 2013).
2. Sanford Levinson, *Constitutional Faith* (Princeton: Princeton University Press, 1988), 116.
3. Edward Coke, *The Third Part of the Institutes of the Laws of England* (London: M. Flesher, 1644), 4–5.
4. *Carlisle v. United States*, 83 U.S. 147 (1872).
5. Ibid., 154.
6. Ibid. (citing Richard Wildman, *Institutes of International Law* [London: William Benning & Co., 1849], 1:40).
7. Matthew Hale, *The History of the Pleas of the Crown* (London: E. & R. Nutt, 1736), 96.
8. *Kawakita v. United States*, 343 U.S. 717 (1952).
9. Ibid., 732–36.
10. See generally Gregg Jones, *Honor in the Dust: Theodore Roosevelt, War in the Philippines, and the Rise and Fall of America's Imperial Dream* (New York: New American Library, 2012).
11. *Downes v. Bidwell*, 182 U.S. 244, 279–80 (1901) (opinion of White, J.).
12. The cases are reported at *United States v. Magtibay*, 2 Phil. 703 (1903); *United States v. Reyes*, 3 Phil. 349 (1904); *United States v. Lagnason*, 3 Phil. 472 (1904).

13. *Lagnason*, 3 Phil. at 494 (Johnson, J., dissenting).
14. *Dorr v. United States*, 195 U.S. 138, 145 (1904). See generally Amy Rossabi, "The Colonial Roots of Criminal Procedure in the Philippines," *Columbia Journal of Asian Law* 11 (1997): 175–211; Andrew Kent, "The Jury and Empire: The *Insular Cases* and the Anti-Jury Movement in the Gilded Age and Progressive Era," *Southern California Law Review* 91 (2018): 375–465.
15. An act temporarily to provide revenue for the Philippine Islands, and other purposes, chap. 140, § 9, 32 Stat. 54–55 (1902); *Magtibay*, 2 Phil. at 705; *Reyes*, 3 Phil. at 352–53.
16. On the legal status of American Samoa, see "Developments in the Law—American Samoa and the Citizenship Clause: A Study in *Insular Cases* Revisionism," *Harvard Law Review* 130 (2017): 1680–1703; on the legal status of American nationals more generally, see Rose Cuison Villazor, "American Nationals and Interstitial Citizenship," *Fordham Law Review* 85 (2017): 1673–1724. In December 2019, a federal district court in Utah held that American Samoans are U.S. citizens under the Constitution. *Fitisemanu v. U.S.*, 2019 WL 6766502 (D. Utah 2019). The federal government has filed an appeal of the decision.
17. 8 U.S.C. § 1101(22).
18. F. Murray Greenwood, "Judges and Treason Law in Lower Canada, England, and the United States during the French Revolution," in *Canadian State Trials: Law, Politics, and Security Measures, 1608-1837*, eds. F. Murray Greenwood and Barry Wright (Toronto: University of Toronto Press, 1996), 1:242–95, 266–69.
19. J. M. Bumsted, "Another Look at the Riel Trial for Treason," in *Canadian State Trials: Political Trials and Security Measures, 1840–1914*, eds. Barry Wright and Susan Binnie

(Toronto: University of Toronto Press, 2009), 3:411–50; Jeremy Ravi Mumford, "Why Was Louis Riel, a United States Citizen, Hanged as a Canadian Traitor in 1885?," *Canadian Historical Review* 88 (2007): 237–62.

20. For a recent biography of Joyce, see Colin Holmes, *Searching for Lord Haw-Haw: The Political Lives of William Joyce* (London: Routledge, 2016). The decision of the House of Lords is available in *Joyce v. Director of Public Prosecutions*, *American Journal of International Law* 40 (1946): 663–79; the decision of the Court of Criminal Appeal is available in *Rex v. Joyce*, *American Journal of International Law* 40 (1946): 210–17.
21. *Joyce v. Director of Public Prosecutions*, 670.
22. It is hard to know whether an American court would follow this precedent. Legal scholars have criticized the ruling as resting on a minute technicality, Holmes, *Searching for Lord Haw-Haw*, 383–86; Glanville L. Williams, "The Correlation of Allegiance and Protection," *Cambridge Law Journal* 10 (1948): 54–76, even though it had some arguable support in a passage in Michael Foster's 1762 treatise on treason law. Foster quoted an otherwise unreported judicial decision that an alien could be subject to a treason prosecution for acts committed abroad if he had left behind "family and effects" that remained under the Crown's protection. Foster, *A Report of Some Proceedings*, 185.
23. American citizens living in Canada were tried for treason during the War of 1812, but there do not appear to be any executions. The trials resulted in some significant rulings on allegiance. Paul Romney and Barry Wright, "State Trials and Security Proceedings in Upper Canada during the War of 1812," in *Canadian State Trials*, 1: 379–405.

24. On the allegiance arguments, see McGinty, *John Brown's Trial*, 212–16; Carlton F. W. Larson, "The Forgotten Constitutional Law of Treason and the Enemy Combatant Problem," *University of Pennsylvania Law Review* 154, no. 4 (2006): 863, 885–90.
25. "The Trial of John Brown for Treason and Insurrection, Charleston, Virginia, 1859," *American State Trials*, ed. John D. Lawson (St. Louis: F.H. Thomas Law Book Co., 1916), 6:799.
26. H. J. Eckenrode, *The Revolution in Virginia* (Boston: Houghton Mifflin, 1916), 259.
27. *Scott v. Sanford*, 60 U.S. 393 (1857).
28. "The Trial of John Anthony Copeland and Shields Green for Murder, Charlestown Virginia, 1859," *American State Trials*, 6:809–13; McGinty, *John Brown's Trial*, 236–37. On Copeland, see Steven Lubet, *The "Colored Hero" of Harper's Ferry: John Anthony Copeland and the War Against Slavery* (New York: Cambridge University Press, 2015).
29. "Trump Claims He Will Investigate Google for 'treasonous' China Ties," *Guardian*, July 16, 2019.
30. Blackstone, *Commentaries on the Laws of England*, 1:464.
31. *Commonwealth v. Proprietors of New Bedford Bridge*, 2 Gray 339, 345 (Mass. 1854); see also *Board of Field Officers of South Carolina Troops v. U.S.*, 20 Ct. Cl. 18, 21 (1885) (suggesting that corporations are "incapable of committing treason").
32. *New York Central and Hudson River Railroad Co. v. U.S.*, 212 U.S. 481, 494–95 (1909).
33. The most well-known free speech case is, of course, *Citizens United v. FEC*, 558 U.S. 310 (2010). The Religious Freedom Restoration Act case is *Hobby Lobby v. Burwell*,

134 S. Ct. 2751 (2014). For an overview, see Adam Winkler, *We the Corporations: How American Businesses Won Their Civil Rights* (New York: Liveright, 2018).

34. Winkler, *We the Corporations*, 103–108.
35. *Afroyim v. Rusk* 387 U.S. 253 (1967).
36. 8 U.S.C. § 1481(a).
37. See generally United States Department of Justice, Office of Legal Counsel, Survey of the Law of Expatriation (2002), available at https://www.justice.gov/sites/default/files/olc/opinions/2002/06/31/op-olc-v026-p0056_0.pdf.
38. 8 U.S.C. § 1481(a)(3).
39. 8 U.S.C. § 1481(a)(7).

8: THE UNLAWFUL EXECUTION OF HIPOLITO SALAZAR

The leading account of the 1847 treason trials by a legal scholar is Laura Gómez, *Manifest Destinies: The Making of the Mexican American Race* (New York: NYU Press, 2007), chapter 1. The best account of the Taos revolt by a historian is James A. Crutchfield, *Revolt at Taos: The New Mexican and Indian Insurrection of 1847* (Yardley, PA: Westholme, 2015). Other works discussing the trials include James A. Crutchfield, *Tragedy at Taos: The Revolt of 1847* (Plano, TX: Republic of Texas Press, 1995); Stephen G. Hyslop, *Bound for Santa Fe: The Road to New Mexico and the American Conquest, 1806–1848* (Norman, OK: University of Oklahoma Press, 2002); *Taos 1847: The Revolt in Contemporary Accounts*, ed. Michael McNierney (Boulder, CO: Johnson Publishing, 1980); Robert J. Tórrez, "The New Mexican 'Revolt' and Treason Trials of 1847," in *Sunshine and Shadows in New Mexico's Past*, ed. Richard Melzer (Los Ranchos, NM: Rio Grande Books 2010), 1:211–34; Robert J. Tórrez, "Revolt of 1847 Treason Trials," New Mexico History, July 8,

2015, http://newmexicohistory.org/2015/07/08/revolt-of-1847-treason-trials-d48/. An older but still useful account is Ralph Emerson Twitchell, *The History of the Military Occupation of the Territory of New Mexico from 1846 to 1851* (Denver, CO: Smith-Brooks, 1909). The Taos court records are reprinted in Francis T. Cheetham, "The First Term of the American Court in Taos, New Mexico," *New Mexico Historical Review* 1 (1926): 23–41. The only surviving eyewitness account of the trials is in Lewis H. Garrard, *Wah-to-yah and the Taos Trail* (Cincinnati: H.W. Derby, 1850).

1. Lewis H. Garrard, *Wah-to-yah and the Taos Trail* (Cincinnati: H.W. Derby, 1850), 195–96, 201.
2. Ibid., 225; Francis T. Cheetham, "The First Term of the American Court in Taos, New Mexico," *New Mexico Historical Review* 1 (1926): 23–41. A map of key locations is provided in James A. Crutchfield, *Revolt at Taos: The New Mexican and Indian Insurrection of 1847* (Yardley, PA: Westholme, 2015), 76–77.
3. James Willard Hurst, *Law of Treason*, 187.
4. William A. Blair, *With Malice toward Some: Treason and Loyalty in the Civil War Era* (Chapel Hill, UNC Press, 2014), 13.
5. Carlton F. W. Larson, "Five Myths About Treason," *Washington Post*, February 17, 2017.
6. Some expansive interpretations of the borders of the Republic of Texas suggested that Taos was part of Texas. However, U.S. officials consistently acted as if Taos was part of the Republic of Mexico. Crutchfield, *Revolt at Taos*, 7, 14.
7. David Herbert Donald, *Lincoln* (New York: Simon & Schuster, 1995), 123–25.

8. Ulysses S. Grant, *Personal Memoirs of U. S. Grant* (Cambridge, MA: Da Capo, 2001), 22–23.
9. Quoted in Ralph Emerson Twitchell, *The History of the Military Occupation of the Territory of New Mexico from 1846 to 1851* (Denver, CO: Smith-Brooks, 1909), 73–74.
10. Stephen Watt Kearny, Proclamation to the People of Santa Fe, August 22, 1846, in Crutchfield, *Revolt at Taos*, 169–70.
11. Laura Gómez, *Manifest Destinies: The Making of the Mexican American Race* (New York: NYU Press, 2007), 25–31.
12. Ibid., 23–24. For the text of the Kearny Code, see https://avalon.law.yale.edu/19th_century/kearney.asp.
13. Frank T. Blair to John Y. Mason, April 1, 1847, in Message of the President of the United States, July 24, 1848, U.S. Congressional Serial Set, Exec. Doc. No. 70 (30th Congress, 1848), 26–27.
14. Blair to Mason, April 1, 1847, 26. Blair's letter states, somewhat confusingly, "four conspicuous persons in the late rebellion were indicted for treason by the grand jury; three put upon their trial, one of whom was found guilty and sentenced by the court, one discharged under a nolle presequi, and two obtained continuance to the adjourned term of the court in May next." It appears that three of the other men indicted for treason were later tried, but the cases ended in hung juries and charges were dropped. Robert J. Tórrez, "The New Mexican 'Revolt' and Treason Trials of 1847," in *Sunshine and Shadows in New Mexico's Past*, ed. Richard Melzer (Los Ranchos, NM: Rio Grande Books 2010), 222.
15. The full indictment is in Twitchell, *History of the Military Occupation*, 140–41.

16. Ibid., 142.
17. Donaciano Vigil to James Buchanan, March 23, 1847, in Message of the President of the United States, 24–25.
18. Ibid.
19. W. L. Marcy to Sterling Price, June 11, 1847, in Message of the President of the United States, 31–33. As Senator Thomas Hart Benton later recalled, Polk may have been concerned that issuing a pardon would have admitted the "legality of the condemnation," but Trujillo had been tried by "some sort of court which had no jurisdiction of treason." Thomas Hart Benton, *Thirty Years' View: A History of the Working of the American Government for Thirty Years from 1820 to 1850* (New York: D. Appleton, 1856), 683.
20. Cheetham, "First Term of the American Court," 27–41. Cheetham's transcription of the court records gives the acquitted defendant's name as "Francisco Revali," which seems likely to be an error. James Crutchfield states that the name was "Francisco Rivole." Crutchfield, *Revolt at Taos*, 108. Robert Tórrez states that the name was "Francisco Ulibarri." Tórrez, "The New Mexican 'Revolt,'" 223.
21. Twitchell, *History of the Military Occupation*, 299–300.
22. Blair to Mason, 27.
23. Garrard, *Wah-to-yah*, 197–98.
24. "Correspondence of the Missouri Republican, Santa Fe, New Mexico, March 18, 1847," *Niles National Register*, May 15, 1847, 173–74. The observer's opposition to the treason trials was rooted not in sympathy to the New Mexicans, but in antipathy to the idea of welcoming them into the United States. As he put it, "A country, which, with but few exceptions, is inhabited by ignorant, dishonest, treacherous men; and by women who are believed

scarcely to know what virtue is, beyond its name, is now part of the American Union!"

25. *Congressional Globe*, December 9, 1846, 18–19 (statement of Isaac Holmes of South Carolina).
26. W. L. Marcy to Stephen W. Kearny, January 11, 1847, in Message of the President of the United States, 13–14.
27. W. L. Marcy to Sterling Price, June 26, 1847, in Message of the President of the United States, 33–34.
28. W. L. Marcy to James K. Polk, July 19, 1848, in Message of the President of the United States, 12.
29. The text of the Treaty of Guadalupe Hidalgo can be found at https://avalon.law.yale.edu/19th_century/guadhida.asp.
30. *Fleming v. Page*, 50 U.S. 603, 615–16 (1850). Of course, the American military was the de facto governing power of New Mexico, and it had authority to punish offenders for a whole range of criminal offenses. As the Supreme Court put it in *Fleming*, the Mexican inhabitants "owed to the United States nothing more than the submission and obedience, sometimes called temporary allegiance, which is due from a conquered enemy, when he surrenders to a force which he is unable to resist." Ibid., 615–16. Although the Court used the term "temporary allegiance," it was doing so loosely, referring to the fact that the Mexican inhabitants could be tried for murder and other crimes. It was not the temporary allegiance that could justify a treason prosecution, which involved noncitizens voluntarily choosing to enter a foreign country and thereby temporarily submitting themselves to that country's authority. By contrast, as the Court elaborated in *Fleming*, until a peace treaty was signed, the Mexicans were "still foreigners and enemies." And persons who are "foreigners and

enemies" do not owe allegiance to the United States (see chapter 10).

31. Message of the President of the United States, July 24, 1848, U.S. Congressional Serial Set, Exec. Doc. No. 70 (30th Congress, 1848).
32. Twitchell, *History of the Military Occupation*, 368–69; Grant, *Memoirs*, 300.
33. Genealogical information was gathered by Karen Mitchell, and is available at http://www.kmitch.com/Taos/revolt1847.html. Some sources suggest that Salazar was not the only person executed for treason. For example, Secretary of War Marcy wrote that "the trials proceeded and resulted in the conviction and execution of several of the accused." W. L. Marcy to James K. Polk, July 19, 1848, in Message of the President of the United States, 12. But other than this, and some vague generalizations in other sources, I have located no concrete evidence of any other execution for treason.
34. Garrard, *Wah-to-yah*, 228.

9: THE CASE OF JEFFERSON DAVIS, PRESIDENT OF THE CONFEDERATE STATES OF AMERICA

Two recent books on Jefferson Davis's treason prosecution are Cynthia Nicoletti, *Secession on Trial: The Treason Prosecution of Jefferson Davis* (New York: Cambridge University Press, 2017), and Robert Icenhauer-Ramirez, *Treason on Trial: The United States v. Jefferson Davis* (Baton Rouge: Louisiana State University Press, 2019). The leading biography of Davis is William J. Cooper Jr., *Jefferson Davis, American* (New York: Knopf, 2000), from which I have drawn most of the biographical background. Documents from the case and records of the judicial proceedings can be found in "Case of Jefferson Davis," *Reports of Cases Decided by Chief Justice Chase in the Circuit Court of the United States for the Fourth Circuit, During the Years 1865 to 1869*, ed. Bradley T. Johnson (New York: Diossy & Co., 1876), 1–124. On treason and the Civil War more generally, see William A. Blair, *With Malice toward Some: Treason and Loyalty in the Civil War Era* (Chapel Hill, NC: UNC Press, 2014).

1. Christopher Mele, "Jefferson Davis Statue in New Orleans Is Removed," *New York Times*, May 11, 2017.
2. Alexander Stephens, "'Cornerstone' Speech," March 21, 1861, available at http://teachingamericanhistory.org/library/document/cornerstone-speech/.
3. Historian William Blair notes, "Treason pervaded public discourse. It represents a challenge for a researcher to find a northern newspaper or periodical during any day of the war in which the words 'traitor' and 'treason' *do not* appear as a characterization of the rebels, of political opponents, or of the people suspected of holding divided loyalties in the United States." Blair, *With Malice toward Some*, 1.
4. "To the Breach," *Cincinnati Gazette*, reprinted in *Daily Telegraph*, April 25, 1861.
5. Ulysses S. Grant to Jesse Root Grant, April 21, 1861, *The Papers of Ulysses S. Grant*, ed. John Y. Simon (Carbondale, IL: Southern Illinois University Press, 1969), 2:6, 7.
6. Quoted in Daniel W. Crofts, *Lincoln and the Politics of Slavery: The Other Thirteenth Amendment and the Struggle to Save the Union* (Chapel Hill: UNC Press, 2016), 247.
7. On the Battle Cry of Freedom, see David Guion, "The Battle Cry of Freedom: Best Song of the Civil War?," Musicology for Everyone, July 30, 2012, http://music.allpurpose

guru.com/2012/07/the-battle-cry-of-freedom-best-song-of-the-civil-war/.

8. Thomas McKean to William Augustus Atlee, June 5, 1778, in *Letters of Delegates to Congress*, ed. Paul H. Smith (Washington, DC: Library of Congress, 1983), 10:31–33.
9. Grant, *Personal Memoirs of U. S. Grant*, 557. On the surrender, see Jay Winik, *April 1865: The Month That Saved America* (New York: HarperCollins, 2001), 173–99.
10. Quoted in William A. Blair, *Why Didn't the North Hang Some Rebels?: The Postwar Debate over Punishment for Treason* (Milwaukee: Marquette University Press, 2004), 8–9.
11. Quoted in ibid., 9.
12. "John Brown's Song," *San Francisco Bulletin*, April 10, 1862.
13. Andrew Johnson, "Speech to the Indiana Delegation," April 21, 1865, in *Papers of Andrew Johnson*, ed. Leroy P. Graf (Knoxville, TN: University of Tennessee Press, 1986), 7:612.
14. "Case of Jefferson Davis," *Official Opinions of the Attorneys General of the United States* (Washington, DC: W.H. and O.H. Morrison, 1869), 11:411–13.
15. Cynthia Nicoletti, *Secession on Trial: The Treason Prosecution of Jefferson Davis* (New York: Cambridge University Press, 2017), 172–81.
16. *The Prize Cases*, 67 U.S. 635 (1863).
17. "Case of Jefferson Davis," *Reports of Cases Decided by Chief Justice Chase in the Circuit Court of the United States for the Fourth Circuit, During the Years 1865 to 1869*, ed. Bradley T. Johnson (New York: Diossy & Co., 1876), 117–18.
18. Nicoletti, *Secession on Trial*, 242–65.
19. "Case of Jefferson Davis," *Official Opinions*, 11:411–13.
20. Nicoletti, *Secession on Trial*, 270–71.

21. Ibid., 294.
22. "Case of Jefferson Davis," *Chase's Reports*, 101–102.
23. Information on Beauvoir can be found at http://www.visitbeauvoir.org/.
24. Craig Fehrman, "Jefferson Davis' 'Presidential' Library," *Los Angeles Times*, June 2, 2013.
25. Theodore Roosevelt, "The President's Policy," *North American Review* 141 (Oct. 1885): 388–96, 393. Roosevelt repeated the charge in his 1887 book *The Life of Thomas Hart Benton* (Boston: Houghton Mifflin, 1887), 163, 220.
26. Quoted in William J. Cooper Jr., *Jefferson Davis, American* (New York: Knopf, 2000), 625.

10: WHO ARE ENEMIES OF THE UNITED STATES?

1. *United States v. Greathouse*, 26 F. Cas. 18, 22 (C.C.N.D. Cal. 1863) (No. 15,254); see also Blackstone, *Commentaries on the Laws of England*, 4:82–83 (for purposes of treason law, "enemies" are "the subjects of foreign powers with whom we are at open war").
2. *United States v. Fricke*, 259 F. 673, 681 (S.D.N.Y. 1919).
3. Foster, *A Report of Some Proceedings*, 219.
4. 1 Op. Att. Gen. 84 (1798). In 1800, the United States Supreme Court unanimously determined in *Bas v. Tingy* (4 U.S. 37) that the term "enemy" in a federal statute applied to France. The justices each delivered individual opinions, but a majority distinguished between solemn, or perfect, wars (which involve complete warfare between the two countries), and limited, or imperfect, wars (which involved lesser degrees of hostility). The dispute with France was a limited war, because it applied only to naval operations. Nonetheless, France was clearly an enemy with respect to

these operations. As Justice Bushrod Washington (George Washington's nephew) explained, French vessels "were certainly not friends, because there was a contention by force; nor were they private enemies, because the contention was external, and authorized by the legitimate authority of the two governments. If they were not our enemies, I know not what constitutes an enemy." Ibid., 41. Although technically this decision applied only to the interpretation of a federal statute, a similar interpretation may apply to the term "enemy" in the Treason Clause.

5. Although no formal treason charges were filed during these conflicts, two federal courts assumed that aid to the North Koreans during the Korean War constituted treason. *Martin v. Young*, 134 F.Supp. 204, 207 (D.N.D. Cal. 1955); *Thompson v. Whittier*, 185 F.Supp. 306, 314 (D.D.C. 1960).
6. *United States v. Fricke*, 259 F. 673, 677 (S.D.N.Y. 1919); see also *United States v. Stephan*, 50 F.Supp. 738, 742, n.1 (E.D. Mich. 1943) ("To constitute treason . . . it is also necessary that it be done in time of war, because that other country must be an enemy country.")
7. For accounts of Americans who have engaged in potentially disloyal actions, but which are not technically treasonous, see Jeremy Duda, *If This Be Treason: The American Rogues and Rebels Who Walked the Line Between Dissent and Betrayal* (Guilford, CT: Globe Pequot, 2017).
8. See, e.g., Ronald Radosh and Joyce Milton, *The Rosenberg File*, 2nd ed. (New Haven: Yale University Press, 1997).
9. Quoted in ibid., 173.
10. Quoted in ibid., 269.
11. Quoted in ibid., 284.
12. On Ames, see Ben Macintyre, *The Spy and the Traitor:*

The Greatest Espionage Story of the Cold War (New York: Crown, 2018).

13. Carlton F. W. Larson, "Sorry, Donald Trump Jr. Is Not a Traitor," *Washington Post*, July 11, 2017. I preferred the headline, "Donald Trump Jr., Is Not a Traitor, but . . ."
14. Jane Mayer, "The Man Behind the Dossier: How Christopher Steele Compiled His Secret Report on Trump's Ties with Russia," *New Yorker*, March 12, 2018, 55.
15. Foster, *A Report of Some Proceedings*, 219. In 1838, Canada was confronted with groups of American citizens who were invading the country, and the issue of their legal status generated considerable discussion. F. Murray Greenwood, "The Prince Affair: 'Gallant Colonel' or 'The Windsor Butcher'?," in *Canadian State Trials: Rebellion and Invasion in the Canadas, 1837–1839*, eds. F. Murray Greenwood and Barry Wright (Toronto: University of Toronto Press, 2002), 2:160–87.
16. Blackstone, *Commentaries on the Laws of England*, 4:83.
17. Thomas McKean, Notes of Charges Delivered to Grand Juries, 1777–1779, Thomas McKean Papers, Historical Society of Pennsylvania, 29.
18. Authorization for Use of Military Force, Pub. L. No. 107-40, 115 Stat. 224 (2001).
19. See chapter 14.
20. *New York Times Co. v. U.S. Dep't of Justice,* 915 F.Supp.2d 508, 522–23 (S.D.N.Y. 2013). This statement is what lawyers call "dicta," meaning a statement that is not necessary to the resolution of the issue in front of the court, which, in this case, dealt with a Freedom of Information Act request.
21. Statement by the President on Progress in the Fight

Against ISIL, April 13, 2016, available at https://obama whitehouse.archives.gov/the-press-office/2016/04/13 /statement-president-progress-fight-against-isil.

22. See generally Larson, "Forgotten Constitutional Law of Treason," 863, 920–23.
23. *Verano v. De Angelis Coal Co.*, 41 F.Supp. 954, 955 (M.D. Pa. 1941).
24. For the details on Russian interference in the 2016 election, see Robert Mueller, *The Mueller Report* (2019), vol. 1, available at https://www.justice.gov/storage/report.pdf.
25. This scenario implicates complicated issues of international law. See Ryan Goodman, "Cyber Operations and the U.S. Definition of 'Armed Attack,'" Just Security, March 8, 2018, https://www.justsecurity.org/53495/cyber-operations-u-s-definition-armed-attack/.
26. Foster, *A Report of Some Proceedings*, 196–97. A similar point had been in the posthumously published treatise by seventeenth-century jurist Sir Matthew Hale, who concluded that "if a subject of the king of England solicits by letters the king of France to invade this realm . . . [i]t is certainly an overt-act to prove treason in compassing the king's death, but it seems not an overt-act to convict him of adhering to the king's enemies." Hale, *History of the Pleas of the Crown*, 1:167. A Canadian judge stated the same principle in 1838: "But the offence of merely inciting foreigners to invade this Province, if those foreigners belong to a country at peace with us, can only be treason as an overt act of compassing the Queen's death." Charge of Chief Justice Robinson to the Grand Jury, Delivered at Toronto, March 8, 1838, in *Canadian State Trials*, 2:464, 467.

27. In the Aaron Burr case, Chief Justice Marshall explained, "All those who perform the various and essential military parts of prosecuting the war . . . may with correctness and accuracy be said to levy war. . . . [T]his opinion does not extend to the case of a person who performs no act in the prosecution of the war—who counsels or advises it—or who, being engaged in the conspiracy, fails to perform his part." *United States v. Burr*, 25 F. Cas. 55, 161 (C.C.D. Va. 1807) (No. 14,693) (Marshall, C.J.).
28. Blackstone, *Commentaries on the Laws of England*, 4:100–101.

11: TOKYO ROSE AND THE WORLD WAR II RADIO BROADCASTERS

The leading studies of the Iva Toguri case are Frederick P. Close, *Tokyo Rose/An American Patriot: A Dual Biography*, rev. ed. (Lanham, MD: Rowman & Littlefield, 2014); Yasuhide Kawashima, *The Tokyo Rose Case: Treason on Trial* (Lawrence, KS: University Press of Kansas, 2013); Masayo Duus, *Tokyo Rose: Orphan of the Pacific* (Tokyo: Kodansha Int'l, 1979); and Rex Gunn, *They Called Her Tokyo Rose* (self-pub., Rex Gunn, 1977). The Ninth Circuit's decision in her appeal is reported at *D'Aquino v. United States*, 192 F.2d 338 (9th Cir. 1951). For a legal analysis of the case, see Stanley I. Kutler, "Forging a Legend: The Treason of Tokyo Rose," *Wisconsin Law Review* (1980): 1341–82.

1. Anthony J. Rudel, *Hello, Everybody! The Dawn of American Radio* (New York: Harcourt, 2008), 33.
2. On technology and the military, see Max Boot, *War Made New: Technology, Warfare, and the Course of History 1500 to Today* (New York: Penguin, 2006).
3. Testimony of head of the U.S.A. Zone, German Radio

Broadcasting Corporation, quoted in *Chandler v. United States*, 171 F.2d 921, 927 (1st Cir. 1948).

4. Yasuhide Kawashima, *The Tokyo Rose Case: Treason on Trial* (Lawrence, KS: University Press of Kansas, 2013), 9–10; Frederick P. Close, *Tokyo Rose/An American Patriot: A Dual Biography*, rev. ed. (Lanham, MD: Rowman & Littlefield, 2014), 33–56.
5. Kawashima, *Tokyo Rose Case*, 10.
6. Close, *Tokyo Rose*, 57.
7. Kawashima, *Tokyo Rose Case*, 12–18; Masayo Duus, *Tokyo Rose: Orphan of the Pacific* (Tokyo: Kodansha Int'l, 1979), 45–54. Toguri was far from alone in this predicament. It is estimated that between seven and ten thousand people born in the United States found themselves trapped in Japan at the outbreak of the war. Duus, *Tokyo Rose*, 107.
8. Close, *Tokyo Rose*, 90.
9. Ibid., 83–84.
10. Ibid., 153–75; Kawashima, *Tokyo Rose Case*, 27–35.
11. Quoted in Duus, *Tokyo Rose*, 80–81.
12. Close, *Tokyo Rose*, 157.
13. Ibid., 1–8.
14. Quoted in ibid., 2. Some of the attributes of "Tokyo Rose" were more properly attributed to "Manila Rose" who broadcast from the Philippines in 1944. Ibid., 163.
15. The contract is reprinted in Duus, *Tokyo Rose*, 22–23.
16. Close, *Tokyo Rose*, 247–48.
17. Nathan T. Elliff to Theron L. Caudle, May 15, 1946, quoted in ibid., 279.
18. Nathan T. Elliff to Theron L. Caudle, Sept. 19, 1946, quoted in Stanley I. Kutler, "Forging a Legend: The Treason of Tokyo Rose," *Wisconsin Law Review* (1980): 1341–82, 1353.

19. DeWolfe's memorandum is reprinted in Rex Gunn, *They Called Her Tokyo Rose* (self-pub., Rex Gunn, 1977), 45–49.
20. Chandler's case is reported at *Chandler v. United States*, 171 F.2d 921 (1st Cir. 1948). A Chandler broadcast from September 1941 can be heard at https://archive.org/details/PropagandaBroadcastByPaulRevere. Although this broadcast pre-dates the war with the United States, and thus was not technically an overt act of treason, it is typical of the later broadcasts.
21. Best's case is reported at *Best v. United States*, 184 F.2d 131 (1st Cir. 1950). One of Best's broadcasts can be heard at https://www.youtube.com/watch?v=isZ8ywQGdWs.
22. The most thorough account of Gillars's life is Richard Lucas, *Axis Sally: The American Voice of Nazi Germany* (Philadelphia: Casemate, 2010).
23. Ibid., 257, 264, 267, 269, 270.
24. Gillars's case is reported at *Gillars v. United States*, 192 F.2d 962 (D.C. Cir. 1950). In a later case, Herbert John Burgman was also convicted for broadcasting for Nazi Germany. See *Burgman v. United States*, 188 F.2d 637 (D.C. Cir. 1951).
25. The scripts of the broadcasts are published in *"Ezra Pound Speaking": Radio Speeches of World War II*, ed. Leonard W. Doob (Westport, CT: Greenwood Press, 1978).
26. Ibid., 289
27. Ibid., 298.
28. On the treason case against Pound, see Robert Spoo, introduction to *Ezra and Dorothy Pound: Letters in Captivity, 1945–1946*, eds. Omar Pound and Robert Spoo (New York: Oxford University Press, 1999), 1–36. Documents from the case are reprinted in Julien Cornell, *The Trial of Ezra Pound: A Documented Account of the Treason Case by*

the Defendant's Lawyer (New York: John Day, 1966); and in Charles Norman, *The Case of Ezra Pound* (New York: Funk & Wagnalls, 1968).

29. Judge Milton Hirsch, for example, concludes that "it is difficult to envision any defense at a trial on the merits that could have resulted in—could even have any hope of resulting in—an acquittal." Milton Hirsch, "'Till the Detail of Surface Is in Accord with the Root in Justice': Treason, Insanity, and the Trial of Ezra Pound," *St. Thomas Law Review* 25 (2013): 143, 153.
30. Duus, *Tokyo Rose*, 184.
31. For example, "Hello, hello again, once again, to all my favorite friends. Here is Orphan Anne with some of that stuff some people label propaganda." Or, "Greetings, Everybody! How are my victims this evening? All ready for a vicious assault on your morale?" For these and other excerpts from the scripts, see Close, *Tokyo Rose*, 167–70.
32. Kawashima, *Tokyo Rose Case*, 61.
33. *Cramer v. United States*, 325 U.S. 1, 34 (1945).
34. The witness statements are in Close, *Tokyo Rose*, 327.
35. Quoted in ibid., 474.
36. Ibid., 335–37.
37. Kawashima, *Tokyo Rose Case*, 82.
38. *Batson v. Kentucky,* 476 U.S. 79 (1986).
39. *D'Aquino v. United States*, 192 F.2d, 338, 363 n.14 (9th Cir. 1951).
40. Close, *Tokyo Rose*, 418.
41. Ibid., 428.
42. Ibid., 480.
43. Ezra Pound to Francis Biddle, August 4, 1943, in *Ezra and Dorothy Pound*, 368–69.

44. Lucas, *Axis Sally*, 120.
45. *Chandler*, 171 F.2d at 938–39.
46. The same argument was rejected by a federal court in World War I: "Letters written, or oral messages sent, to convey information of value to an enemy, could not be deemed otherwise than as treasonable, whether the former were sent by post or telegraph, and the latter by a messenger or a shout." *United States v. Werner*, 247 F. 708, 711 (E.D. Pa. 1918).
47. Ibid., 939; see also *Gillars*, 192 F.2d at 971.
48. Although the Supreme Court permitted the suppression of antiwar speech during World War I on the theory that it might encourage soldiers to desert, those decisions have long since been reversed. Speech in favor of the enemy in wartime is now governed by the Supreme Court's 1969 decision in *Brandenburg v. Ohio*, 395 U.S. 444 (1969). Under this decision, government may not "forbid or proscribe advocacy of the use of force or of law violation except where such advocacy is directed to inciting or producing imminent lawless action and is likely to incite or produce such action." Ibid., 447.

    This is a stringent standard, and it means that almost any propaganda effort by a person in the United States on behalf of foreign enemies will be protected by the First Amendment, for the simple reason that such propaganda is unlikely to lead to any imminent violation of the law. If *Brandenburg* governed speech that is directly coordinated with the enemy, the World War II broadcasters would have a strong claim, given that their speech was equally unlikely to lead to imminent violations of the law.

But modern courts are likely to agree with the World War II decisions that trafficking with the enemy is wholly outside the protection of the First Amendment. In the most relevant recent case, the Supreme Court rejected a free speech challenge brought by groups that sought to provide training services to entities designated as foreign terrorist organizations. In *Holder v. Humanitarian Aid Project*, the Court held that "advocacy performed in coordination with, or at the direction of, a foreign terrorist organization" could be prohibited. By contrast, the Court stated, "we in no way suggest that a regulation of independent speech would pass constitutional muster, even if the Government were to show that such speech benefits foreign terrorist organizations." 561 U.S. 1, 24, 31–32, 36, 39 (2010). Although four justices expressed doubts about such a dividing line, even they conceded that the government could restrict speech if it could show that the defendants "provided support that they knew was significantly likely to help the organization pursue its unlawful terrorist aims," a standard that would easily encompass serving as an enemy broadcaster. Ibid., 56 (Breyer, J., dissenting); see also ibid., 57 ("[T]he act of providing material support to a known terrorist organization bears a close enough relationship to terrorist acts that, in my view, it likely can be prohibited notwithstanding any First Amendment interest.").

12: WHAT IS "ADHERING TO THE ENEMY, GIVING IT AID AND COMFORT"?

There are few extensive discussions of what actions constitute providing aid and comfort to the enemy. The one law review article devoted solely to this topic is Charles Warren, "What Is Giving Aid and Comfort to the Enemy?," *Yale Law Journal* 27 (1918): 331–47. Several of Warren's conclusions were overly broad even in 1918, and many of his premises were rejected in the *Cramer* decision in 1945. For a full historical account of the *Cramer* case, see J. Woodford Howard Jr., "Advocacy in Constitutional Choice: The *Cramer* Treason Case, 1942–1945," *American Bar Foundation Research Journal* (1986): 375–413.

1. *United States v. Fricke,* 259 F. 673, 676 (S.D.N.Y. 1919).
2. *Kawakita v. United States*, 343 U.S. 717, 737 (1952) ("a long, persistent, and continuous course of conduct directed against the American prisoners and going beyond any conceivable duty of an interpreter").
3. *Chandler v. United States*, 171 F.2d 921 (1st Cir. 1948); *Gillars v. United States*, 192 F.2d 962 (D.C. Cir. 1950); *Best v. United States*, 184 F.2d 131 (1st Cir. 1950); *D'Aquino v. United States,* 192 F.2d 338 (9th Cir. 1951); *Burgman v. United States*, 188 F.2d 637 (D.C. Cir. 1951).
4. *Haupt v. United States*, 67 U.S. 874 (1947).
5. *Stephan v. United States*, 133 F.2d 87 (6th Cir. 1943).
6. *Kawakita v. United States*, 343 U.S. 717, 734 (1952).
7. Ibid., 738–41.
8. *Cramer v. United States*, 325 U.S. 1, 1–6 (1945).
9. Ibid., 34.
10. Ibid., 34.
11. Ibid., 34–35.
12. Ibid., 61 (Douglas, J., dissenting).
13. Ibid., 67 (Douglas, J., dissenting).
14. Ibid., 39.
15. Paul T. Crane, "Did the Court Kill the Treason Charge?:

Reassessing *Cramer v. United States* and Its Significance," *Florida State University Law Review* 36 (2009): 635, 678.

16. *Haupt*, 67 U.S. at 876.
17. *Kawakita*, 343 U.S. at 741.
18. Foster, *A Report of Some Proceedings*, 217.
19. *United States v. Greathouse*, 26 F. Cas. 18, 23–24 (C.C.N.D. Cal. 1863) (No. 15,254) (Field, J.).
20. *Respublica v. Malin*, 1 U.S. (1 Dallas) 33, 33–34 (Pa. Ct. Oyer & Terminer, 1778); on the Malin case, see Larson, *Trials of Allegiance*, 117–21.
21. *Cramer*, 325 U.S. at 34 (emphasis added).
22. Ibid., 34 n.44.
23. See Hurst, *Law of Treason*, 207–10. Hurst argued, "To wait for aid to be 'actually' given the enemy risks stultification: the treason may be successful to the point at which there will no longer be a sovereign to punish it." Ibid., 210.
24. See, e.g., Charge to Grand Jury—Treason, 30 F. Cas. 1034, 1036 (C.C.S.D.N.Y. 1861) (No. 18,271) (Nelson, J.) (trade with the enemy is treason "if carried on for the purpose and with the intent of giving aid and assistance to the enemy in their hostility against the government").
25. 50 U.S.C. §4301 et seq.

13: THE REQUIREMENT OF TRAITOROUS INTENT

1. Dylan Matthews, "No, Edward Snowden Probably Didn't Commit Treason," *Washington Post* Wonkblog, June 12, 2013.
2. Andrew Blake, "Edward Snowden on Ted Cruz Debate Slam: 'Treason Only If the Voter Is Your Enemy,'" *Washington Times*, March 4, 2016.
3. See chapter 10.

4. Richard Spencer, "US Withdrawal 'Facilitated the Escape of Isis Fighters,'" *Times*, October 24, 2019.
5. Jane Fonda, *My Life So Far* (New York: Random House, 2005), 315–18.
6. Quoted in Colby Itkowitz, "How Jane Fonda's 1972 Trip to North Vietnam Earned Her the Nickname 'Hanoi Jane,'" *Washington Post*, September 18, 2017.
7. Fonda, *My Life So Far*, 291.
8. See generally Wayne R. LaFave, *Substantive Criminal Law*, 3rd ed. (Eagan, MN: Thomson West, 2017), 1:§5; Markus D. Dubber, *An Introduction to the Model Penal Code*, 2nd ed. (New York: Oxford University Press, 2015), 35–69.
9. The Supreme Court explicitly stated that "negligent" acts could not amount to treason. *Cramer v. United States*, 325 U.S. 1, 31 (1945). It has also stated that one may "commit acts which do give aid and comfort to the enemy and yet not be guilty of treason, as for example where he acts impulsively with no intent to betray." *Kawakita v. United States*, 343 U.S. 717, 736 (1952). This suggests that reckless behavior does not satisfy the constitutional requirement.
10. *Chandler v. United States*, 171 F.2d 921, 943 (1st Cir. 1948) (quoting jury instructions). This is a close paraphrase of language in *Cramer* that states, "The law of treason, like the law of lesser crimes, assumes every man to intend the natural consequences which one standing in his circumstances and possessing his knowledge would reasonably expect to result from his acts." 325 U.S. at 31.
11. One treatise, for example, asserts that treason "requires the doing of something with the purpose of aiding the enemy." Dubber, *Model Penal Code*, 55.

12. *Cramer v. United States*, 325 U.S. 1, 31 (1945).
13. Ibid., 29.
14. *Haupt v. United States*, 330 U.S. 631, 641 (1947).
15. The case is explored in depth in Eric L. Muller, "Betrayal on Trial: Japanese-American Treason in World War II," *North Carolina Law Review* 82 (2004): 1759–98.
16. Quoted in ibid., 1785.
17. *United States v. Stephan*, 50 F.Supp. 738, 744 n.1 (E.D. Mich. 1943).
18. *Stephan v. United States*, 133 F.2d 87 (6th Cir. 1943).
19. *United States v. Werner*, 247 F. 708, 710 (E.D. Pa. 1918).
20. Hale, *History of the Pleas of the Crown*, 1:169.
21. *Chandler v. U.S.*, 171 F.2d 921, 943–44 (1st Cir. 1948).
22. Ibid., 943.
23. The texts of the broadcasts can be found in *Hearings Before the Committee on Internal Security, House of Representatives, 92d Congress, 2d Session* (Washington, DC: U.S. Government Printing Office, 1972), 7644–71.
24. Ibid., 7655.
25. Fonda, *My Life So Far*, 314.
26. For a strident statement of the case against Fonda, see Henry Mark Holzer and Erika Holzer, *"Aid and Comfort": Jane Fonda in North Vietnam* (Jefferson, NC: McFarland & Co., 2002). The Holzers consider a wider range of Fonda's conduct potentially treasonous, whereas I see the radio broadcasts as the most likely subjects of a treason prosecution.
27. Quoted in Fonda, *My Life So Far*, 323.
28. Jerry Lembcke, *Hanoi Jane: War, Sex & Fantasies of Betrayal* (Amherst, MA: University of Massachusetts Press, 2010), 23–27.

29. Joseph E. Thach, "Compilation of Broadcasts Previously Made over Radio Hanoi by Other U.S. Citizens," in *Hearings Before the Committee*, 7682–83.
30. Lembcke, *Hanoi Jane*, 22.
31. Indeed, the Nixon administration had even considered sending entertainer Bob Hope to Hanoi to perform his revue show as a part of an attempt to gain the release of POWs. Mary Hershberger, *Jane Fonda's War: A Political Biography of an Antiwar Icon* (New York: New Press, 2005), 49.
32. Tim O'Brien, "Ramsey Clark Airings Called 'Contemptible,'" *Washington Post*, August 12, 1972, A7.
33. Fonda, *My Life So Far*, 321.
34. John A. Farrell, "Nixon's Vietnam Treachery," *New York Times*, December 31, 2016.
35. *United States v. Wimmer*, 264 F. 11, 13 (6th Cir. 1920).

14: ADAM GADAHN AND THE WAR ON TERROR

The primary biographical account of Gadahn is Raffi Khatchadourian, "Azzam the American," *New Yorker*, January 22, 2007, 50–63. There are also valuable accounts in the *Orange County Register*, cited on the following pages. Transcripts of Gadahn's videos, letters, and articles can be found in Steven Stalinsky, *American Traitor: The Rise and Fall of Al-Qaeda's U.S.-Born Leader Adam Gadahn* (Washington, DC: MEMRI Books, 2017).

1. Peggy Lowe, "Radical Conversion," *Orange County Register*, September 24, 2006.
2. On Nancy Pearlman's career, see http://www.nancypearlman.net/. Pearlman was a trustee of the Los Angeles Community College District from 2001 to 2017.
3. Peggy Lowe, "Sons in Family Rebelled Against Father's

Ways," *Orange County Register*, September 26, 2006. The family eventually got solar panels for electricity. Raffi Khatchadourian, "Azzam the American," *New Yorker*, January 22, 2007, 52. Adam Gadahn later claimed that the family's surname was based on the Arabic word for "tomorrow." Steven Stalinsky, *American Traitor: The Rise and Fall of Al-Qaeda's U.S.-Born Leader Adam Gadahn* (Washington, DC: MEMRI Books, 2017), 423.

4. Khatchadourian, "Azzam the American," 56–57.
5. Lowe, "Radical Conversion."
6. Theresa Walker and Scott Schwebke, "Local Man Became a Voice of Terror," *Orange County Register*, April 24, 2015.
7. Khatchadourian, "Azzam the American," 58–60.
8. Ibid., 61–62.
9. Ibid., 62.
10. Aldrin Brown and Tony Saavedra, "Report Accuses Gadahn in Plot on U.S.," *Orange County Register*, June 2, 2004.
11. Tony Saavedra, Pat Brennan, Chris Knap, and Natalya Shulyakovskaya, "Area Man's Family Shocked by News," *Orange County Register*, May 27, 2004.
12. Paul T. Crane, "Did the Court Kill the Treason Charge?: Reassessing *Cramer v. United States* and its Significance," *Florida State University Law Review* 36 (2009): 635, 637.
13. *U.S. v. Adam Gadahn*, First Superseding Indictment (C.D. Cal. 2006), available at https://www.justice.gov/sites/default/files/opa/legacy/2006/10/11/adam_indictment.pdf.
14. United States Department of Justice Press Release, "U.S. Citizen Indicted on Treason, Material Support Charges for Providing Aid and Comfort to al Qaeda," October 11, 2006, available at https://www.justice.gov/archive/opa/pr/2006/October/06_nsd_695.html.

15. Vik Jolly, "Treason Charges Filed," *Orange County Register*, Oct. 12, 2006.
16. *New York Times Co. v. U.S. Dep't of Justice,* 915 F.Supp.2d 508, 522–24 (S.D.N.Y. 2013).
17. Testimony of A. William Olson, *Hearings Regarding H.R. 16742: Restraints on Travel to Hostile Areas—Hearings Before the Committee on Internal Security, Ninety-Second Congress, Second Session* (Washington, DC: U.S. Government Printing Office, 1972), 7553–54.
18. For an engaging exploration of this problem, see W. T. Brotherton Jr., "A Case of Treasonous Interpretation," *West Virginia Law Review* 90 (1987): 3–16.
19. Testimony of A. William Olson, 7553–54.
20. Annie Palmer, "Viral Clip That Appears to Show Obama Calling President Trump 'Total and Complete Dips***' and Warning About a 'F****d up Dystopia' Highlights Growing Concerns over 'Deepfakes' Videos," *Daily Mail*, April 18, 2018, http://www.dailymail.co.uk/sciencetech/article-5630775/Viral-deepfakes-video-Barack-Obama-shows-calling-President-Donald-Trump-total-dips.html; Joshua Rothman, "Afterimage," *New Yorker*, November 12, 2018, 34.
21. For more extensive analysis, see Carlton F. W. Larson, "A Difficult Issue," Cato Unbound, June 13, 2011, available at https://www.cato-unbound.org/2011/06/13/carlton-f-w-larson/difficult-issue, and the other essays linked therein.

CONCLUSION

1. Larson, *Trials of Allegiance*, 251.
2. Lucas, *Axis Sally*, 119. In 1942, Max Stephan was sentenced

to death by hanging for aiding a German POW. His sentence was later commuted to life imprisonment.

3. *Cramer v. United States*, 325 U.S. 1, 21 (1945).
4. *Ex parte Bollman*, 8 U.S. 75, 125 (1807).
5. Robert Bolt, *A Man for All Seasons* (New York: Random House, 1962), 66.
6. *Bollman*, 8 U.S. at 126–27.
7. *Cramer*, 325 U.S. at 45–46.
8. Similarly, under Article II of the Constitution, federal executive and judicial officials can be removed from office after impeachment and conviction for "treason, bribery, and other high crimes and misdemeanors." At the heart of the impeachment provision is a deep concern about disloyalty. Treason and bribery are the quintessential examples of officials placing the interests of other countries, or their own personal financial interests, above the interests of America. "Other high crimes and misdemeanors" is a broader phrase, designed to include disloyal actions that may not technically amount to treason or bribery, but are similar enough to warrant removal from office. It is no defense to claim, "Well, it's not technically treason." If members of Congress are willing to take their constitutional duties seriously, impeachment can be a vital check on disloyal governmental officials.

INDEX

ABOUT THE AUTHOR

CARLTON F. W. LARSON is a Martin Luther King Jr. Professor of Law at the University of California, Davis, School of Law, where he teaches American constitutional law and English and American legal history. A graduate of Harvard College and Yale Law School, Larson is one of the nation's leading authorities on the law of treason. His scholarship has been cited by numerous federal and state courts and has been highlighted in the *New York Times* and many other publications. He is a frequent commentator for the national media on constitutional law issues and is the author of the book *The Trials of Allegiance: Treason, Juries, and the American Revolution.*